ALISSON

MATT AND TOM OLDFIELD

ULTIMATE
FOOTBALL HEROES

ALISSON

FROM THE PLAYGROUND
TO THE PITCH

DINO

First published by Dino Books in 2020,
an imprint of Bonnier Books UK,
The Plaza,
535 Kings Road,
London SW10 0SZ

🐦 @dinobooks
🐦 @footieheroesbks
heroesfootball.com
www.bonnierbooks.co.uk

Text © Matt and Tom Oldfield 2020

Design and typesetting by www.envydesign.co.uk

Paperback ISBN: 9781789462388
E-book ISBN: 9781789462395

British Library Cataloguing-in-Publication Data:
A catalogue record for this book is available from the British Library.

Printed and bound in Great Britain by Clays Ltd, Elcograf S.p.A.

1 3 5 7 9 10 8 6 4 2

For all readers, young and old(er)

ULTIMATE
FOOTBALL HEROES

Matt Oldfield delivers sports writing workshops in schools, and is the author of *Unbelievable Football* and *Johnny Ball: Accidental Football Genius*. Tom Oldfield is a freelance sports writer and the author of biographies on Cristiano Ronaldo, Arsène Wenger and Rafael Nadal.

Cover illustration by Dan Leydon
To learn more about Dan visit danleydon.com
To purchase his artwork visit etsy.com/shop/footynews
Or just follow him on Twitter @danleydon

TABLE OF CONTENTS

ACKNOWLEDGEMENTS

First of all, I'd like to thank Bonnier Books UK –
and particularly my editor Laura Pollard – for sup-
porting me throughout and for running the ever-
expanding UFH ship so smoothly. Writing stories for
the next generation of football fans is both an
honour and a pleasure.

I wouldn't be doing this if it wasn't for my brother
Tom. I owe him so much and I'm very grateful for
his belief in me as an author. I feel like Robin setting
out on a solo career after a great partnership with
Batman. I hope I do him (Tom, not Batman) justice
with these new books.

Next up, I want to thank my friends for keeping

me sane during long hours in front of the laptop.
Pang, Will, Mills, Doug, John, Charlie – the laughs
and the cups of coffee are always appreciated.

I've already thanked my brother but I'm also very
grateful to the rest of my family, especially Melissa,
Noah and of course Mum and Dad. To my parents,
I owe my biggest passions: football and books.
They're a real inspiration for everything I do.

Finally, I couldn't have done this without Iona's
encouragement and understanding during long,
work-filled weekends. Much love to you.

CHAPTER 1

CLUB CHAMPIONS OF THE WORLD!

21 December 2019, Khalifa International
Stadium, Doha

What a year 2019 was turning out to be for
Liverpool. The Reds were already the Champions
of Europe, and now they were just one win away
from becoming Champions of the *World!* Despite
the club's amazing history, that was a title that they
had never achieved before. The players were all
really looking forward to competing in the 2019
FIFA Club World Cup Final – especially their great
goalkeeper, Alisson.

As a boy growing up in Brazil, Alisson had

watched his local team, Internacional, beat the mighty Barcelona to win the tournament in 2006. What a proud and exciting night it had been! He had never forgotten that glorious victory over Ronaldinho and Co, and the way it made him feel as a fan. Ever since then, Alisson had dreamed of lifting that glittering gold trophy himself. Now his opportunity had arrived, and he was ready to catch it in his safe hands and never let go.

'Let's do this!' He clapped and cheered as the two teams emerged onto the pitch in Qatar.

To make things even more exciting for Alisson, Liverpool's opponents in the final were Flamengo, a club from Brazil. And in the Flamengo line-up, there were lots of familiar faces – his old Roma pal Gerson Santos da Silva, plus his national teammates Filipe Luís, Gabriel Barbosa, Diego Alves, Rodrigo Caio…

'Come on, we can't lose to this lot!' Alisson urged his defenders. That fighting spirit, developed all those years ago during his battles with brother Muriel, was what made him such a winner.

Trent Alexander-Arnold, Virgil van Dijk, Joe

Gomez, Andy Robertson… Liverpool had the best back four in the business. But if Flamengo's attackers did somehow manage to get past them, Alisson would be there to save the day as usual.

For the first fifty minutes, however, he didn't have much shot-stopping to do. Liverpool were a team on the attack and their other Brazilian player, Roberto Firmino, missed two great chances to score. He blazed the first one over the bar and then hit the post with the second.

'So close!' Alisson groaned, standing on the edge of his area with his hands on his head.

Even though most of the action was happening at the other end of the pitch, Alisson always stayed alert. He couldn't let his concentration slip, not even for a second. Because as a keeper, you never knew when the ball would come flying towards you…

Suddenly, Éverton Ribeiro flicked it through to Barbosa, who turned and *BANG!* His shot was travelling towards the bottom corner, but down dived Alisson to push it powerfully away. *SAVED!*

What would Liverpool do without their calm and

incredible keeper? As he got back up, Alisson was
already organising his defenders for the corner. He
wanted to win that FIFA Club World Cup trophy
badly, and a clean sheet would be a lovely bonus.

Alisson was looking unbeatable, but unfortunately
so was Diego Alves, the keeper at the other end.
After ninety minutes, it was still 0–0. Would there
be a winner in extra-time, or would Liverpool need
a spot-kick king for a penalty shoot-out?

At last, a goal arrived. The captain Jordan
Henderson played a perfect long pass to Sadio Mané,
who squared it to Roberto inside the Flamengo box.
Surely, he couldn't miss a hat-trick of chances? No,
this time, he kept calm and hit the back of the net.
1–0 to Liverpool!

'Yessss!' Alisson punched the air with pride and
passion, but he knew that the final wasn't over yet.
No, they still had ten minutes of defending to do
first, so they needed to…

'Focus!'

When the final whistle eventually blew, Alisson
threw his arms up in the air and ran over to

celebrate with his Liverpool family – Virgil van Dijk, his manager Jürgen Klopp, and of course, Roberto. What a year it had been for the two of them. They had won the Champions League for their club, then the Copa América for their country, and now this! Liverpool's brilliant Brazilians kissed their latest trophy and carried it proudly around the pitch.

'I'm really happy,' Alisson told the TV cameras, with his winner's medal around his neck and his gloves still on his hands. 'We won the Champions League, and now we're in the race for the Premier League again. But first, we need to enjoy this moment – we're Club Champions of the World!'

CHAPTER 2

A FAMILY OF CRAZY KEEPERS

Sometimes, a job can become a family tradition, passed from generation to generation. For example, you might find a long family line of butchers, or doctors, or shopkeepers, or teachers.

Once upon a time, the Beckers of Novo Hamburgo, Brazil, had been a family of bakers, but now they were a family of goalkeepers instead.

The great-grandfather, Gustavo, had played in goal for the local amateur football club.

The mother, Magali, had played in goal for her handball team at school.

The father, José Agostinho, played in goal for his work football team.

The elder son, Muriel, was already a promising young goalkeeper in the academy of the top local club, Sport Club Internacional.

And the younger son? Well, what choice did Alisson have? He was surrounded by crazy keepers! It seemed like everywhere he looked, there were Beckers wearing gloves and throwing themselves across the goal.

'Cool, that looks like fun!' young Alisson thought to himself.

By the age of five, he was just as crazy about football as the rest of his family. Well, almost. No-one was more passionate than Alisson's dad, especially when the Brazil national team was playing.

'Come on, that's it – ATTACK! SCORE!' José screamed loudly at the TV screen, as if the players on the pitch thousands of miles away could hear him. They couldn't, though, and that just made him scream even louder. Hours after a match, Alisson would still hear his dad's shouts ringing in his ears.

That year, Brazil played in the 1998 World Cup. The *Seleção* had already won the trophy three times before, and all over the country, people were getting ready to celebrate a fourth title. Because who could possibly beat Brazil when they had the best strike force in the world: Rivaldo and Ronaldo?

With the Becker family watching and screaming back in Novo Hamburgo, the *Seleção* topped their group, and then beat Chile and Denmark. Brazil were through to the World Cup semi-finals, which was a great excuse for... a big Becker family party!

Alisson's aunt and uncle agreed to host it, and they put on a huge banquet of delicious foods. His little eyes lit up at all the tasty treats around the table. But where to start? Alisson loved sweet things and he soon spotted an enormous, scrumptious-looking cake.

'Not yet, little man – that's for when we win!' his uncle declared confidently.

After eating way too much of everything (except the cake, of course), Alisson settled down with his family to watch the big game – Brazil vs The Netherlands.

'Yessss!' they all cheered when Ronaldo scored first.

'Noooo!' they all groaned when Patrick Kluivert scored a late equaliser.

It was 1–1 – extra-time! The tension was too much for Alisson's dad and uncle. They couldn't sit still anymore, so instead they spent the next thirty minutes on their feet, pacing up and down the room.

'Hey ref, that's a foul!' they screamed as Rivaldo fell to the floor.

'Hey ref, that's a goal!' they screamed when a Dutch defender cleared Ronaldo's overhead-kick off the line.

But no, the ball wasn't in, and so the semi-final went to penalties. As a family of crazy keepers, the Beckers usually loved watching shoot-outs, but not when their beloved Brazil were involved. It was unbearable!

Alisson was so worried that he put his T-shirt over his face, but then peeked out over the top. 'Good luck!' he muttered to Brazil's brilliant keeper, Cláudio Taffarel.

'I can't watch! I can't watch!' José kept saying,

but he watched every one of Brazil's spot-kicks
go in.

Ronaldo – 'Yes!'

Rivaldo – 'Yes!'

Emerson – 'Yes!'

Dunga – 'Yes!'

As Ronald de Boer stepped up for the
Netherlands, he knew he had to score, otherwise
they were out. He fired the ball powerfully towards
the bottom corner, but Taffarel dived down and
tipped it wide. *SAVED!*

'Yesssss!' the Becker family cheered happily as
their hero dropped to his knees in the mouth of
the goal.

Brazil were through to the World Cup Final, and
José decided that deserved a big celebration. But
what could he do?

A dad dance?

Pull his shirt over his head?

No – instead, Alisson's dad ran over to the table of
food and dunked his face into the cake!

At first, there was a shocked silence across

the room, but when José looked up with his face covered in cake, everyone collapsed into fits of laughter. And Alisson laughed the loudest and longest – it was the funniest thing that he had ever seen – and Magali had to stop him from copying his silly dad.

'Please Mum, I'm hungry!'

But it turned out that Brazil weren't unbeatable, after all. When France won the World Cup Final 3–0, it was a very sad day in the Becker family. Alisson wasn't sure that his dad would ever recover from the disappointment, but by the following week, he was back out on the football pitch, being a crazy keeper again.

'Come on, that's it – DEFEND!' José screamed at his teammates, just like he screamed at the Brazil players on TV.

Alisson and Muriel loved going to watch their dad play. He was a good goalkeeper, but he was also a wild goalkeeper.

If an attacker was running through on goal, José would rush out bravely and dive down at his feet.

If a cross came into the crowded penalty area, José would jump up fearlessly and try to punch the ball away.

It didn't always work, but it was always exciting to watch.

'I want to be just like Dad when I'm older!' young Alisson thought to himself. After all, being a crazy keeper clearly ran in the family.

CHAPTER 3

THE BROTHERLY BATTLES BEGIN

José wasn't the only family member that little Alisson wanted to follow.

'Please let me come with you today!' he begged his older brother Muriel when he went out to play football with his friends in the streets. It looked like so much fun, and he needed to practise his skills.

At first, Muriel said no, but Alisson didn't give up. If he kept asking every day, eventually, his brother would have to say yes.

'Fine, you can come,' Muriel said at last with a grumpy sigh, 'but just don't embarrass me, okay?'

Alisson jumped up and down with excitement. 'Thanks, you're the best brother ever!'

Out in the street, the kids huddled together to pick the teams. Alisson was the youngest and the smallest too. The older boys towered over him like mountains, but he was determined to be fearless like his father.

Alisson didn't complain when he was the last player to be picked, and he didn't complain when his teammates asked him to go in goal either.

'No problem,' Alisson replied with a smile. He was just happy to be playing football, and he was ready to become a crazy keeper like the rest of his family.

As he took his place between the stones that marked out the goal, Alisson saw that Muriel was keeper for the other team. Let the battle of the brothers begin!

It turned out to be a very busy afternoon for Alisson. Muriel's team were much better, and their strikers could really blast the ball hard. The first few shots flew straight past Alisson, but he didn't give up. He just needed to be brave and find a way to stop the other team from scoring.

The next time Muriel's team attacked, Alisson

rushed out bravely like his dad and made himself as big as possible.

'You're not scoring this time!' he thought, looking fiercely at the striker coming his way.

BANG! As the ball came flying towards him, Alisson watched it carefully, all the way. Then, just when it looked like it was going to be another goal, he stuck out his right arm and tipped the shot away.

'Nice one!' his teammates congratulated him. 'You really saved us there!'

On his goal line, Alisson puffed out his chest with pride.

Although his team lost the game, Alisson still walked back home feeling like a winner. He had enjoyed every minute of it, and he had proved that he was good enough to play with Muriel and the big boys. Hopefully, they would let him join in every day now. But Alisson's good mood soon vanished when his brother started teasing him at dinner.

'Yeah, you're not bad...' Muriel began with a wicked grin on his face, '...for a shorty!'

'Hey, don't be mean!' Alisson didn't like it when

people made fun of his size, and his brother knew that. Muriel was an expert at winding him up, and it worked every time. Alisson could feel the angry tears coming.

'Oh, come on. It was only a joke,' Muriel protested as his parents gave him a disappointed look. 'Why do you have to be such a cry baby, bro?'

'I hate you!' Alisson sobbed as he stormed off to his bedroom.

Thankfully, the arguments between the brothers never lasted long. Eventually, Muriel would always come and say sorry, and then they would be best friends again, talking happily about football together. Their parents found it hard to keep up.

'Why do they have to be so competitive with each other all the time?' Magali wondered.

José laughed. 'Sorry, I think they might have got that from me!'

As he got older, Alisson got better at controlling his emotions, and he got better at being a goal-keeper too. He had his brother to thank for both of those things. He learned to ignore Muriel's hurtful comments, but he also learned to copy his keeper skills.

'I want to be as good as him when I'm older!' Alisson thought.

Whenever his brother trained at the Internacional academy, Alisson was there watching on the sidelines. He didn't take notes, but he didn't need to; he could remember every catch, punch, kick and save that Muriel made. Then, when he got home, he would practise them again and again until he could perform them perfectly.

'Anything he can do, I can do too!' Alisson kept telling himself.

Before their brotherly battles had begun, Alisson had dreamed of becoming the next Ronaldo or the next Roberto Carlos. But now, his mind was made up. He wanted to become the next crazy keeper in his family, and then when he was old enough, the next Taffarel, Brazil's brilliant Number 1.

One day, as Muriel and his teammates left the pitch at the end of their session, an Internacional youth coach came over to Alisson, with a ball in his hand.

'Fancy a kickaround?' he suggested.

Alisson's eyes lit up – he had started to think that no-one would ever ask him to play.

'Yes please!' he replied, racing out onto the grass.

At first, they just passed the ball from side to side, but that soon got boring.

'Do you want to take some shots?' the youth coach asked, expecting to hear another eager 'Yes!'.

But Alisson had a better idea: 'No, you can take shots – I'll go in goal!'

28

CHAPTER 4

WORLD CUP WINNERS

Like a lot of kids, Alisson and Muriel loved
sleeping in really late at the weekend, but there
was one thing that they didn't mind getting up
early for: football!

Four years had passed since their silly dad had
dunked his face in that cake. It was now time for
the 2002 World Cup, and it was taking place a
long way away in Asia. There was a twelve-hour
time difference, which meant that if a match kicked
off at 6pm in South Korea, it would be 6am for
the Becker family in Brazil.

'Why does it have to start so early?' Muriel moaned.

But despite their grumbles, Alisson and Muriel

never missed a match. They would be there in front
of the TV every morning, still half-asleep as the next
exciting game kicked off.

'Come on, Brazil!' they called out, while
munching their way through a selection of snacks
for breakfast.

It was a very special tournament for Alisson.
Now that he was nine years old, he understood
so much more about football – the tactics, the
positions, the top players from all over the world.
That knowledge made it all extra exciting.

And it was a very special tournament for the
rest of Brazil too. This time, their national team
were going all the way, no doubt about it. As well
as Ronaldo and Rivaldo, they now had Ronaldinho
and Kaká too. No other nation could compete
with that amazing attack! There would be no
disappointing defeat in the final this time because
Brazil were better than ever. They were going
to win the World Cup for a fourth time, and their
biggest fans, Alisson and Muriel, would be
watching every minute.

'Yes!' they cheered as Rivaldo scored the winner against Turkey.

'Yes!' they cheered as Roberto Carlos fired in a free-kick rocket against China.

'Yes!' they cheered as Júnior added a fifth against Costa Rica.

Three games, three wins, eleven goals scored – the Brazil team looked so strong and settled, except for in one position, perhaps. This was a very important position, especially for the Becker family – the goalkeeper!

The *Seleção's* penalty hero Taffarel had retired after the 1998 World Cup, and now Brazil had three new keepers to choose from:

Rogério Ceni, who played for São Paulo,

Dida, who played for Corinthians,

and Marcos, who played for Palmeiras.

They were all good, solid options, but none of them stood out as a shot-stopping superstar. In the end, the Brazil manager, Luiz Felipe Scolari, had made Marcos his Number 1. Marcos had done a decent job so far, but was he good enough to help them win the World Cup?

Some fans weren't sure of Marcos's potential, but Alisson believed in him. Like Taffarel, Marcos was calm, consistent, and he didn't make many mistakes. That was perfect for a team like Brazil, who dominated every game. When there weren't many shots to save, some keepers switched off and lost their concentration. But not Marcos, and not young Alisson either, who was training himself up to be Brazil's brilliant future Number 1.

For now, Marcos was the man wearing that glorious shirt. And with his country counting on him, his performances got better and better.

With Brazil drawing 0–0 against Belgium in the Round of 16, Marcos stretched across his goal to tip Marc Wilmots's strike around the post.

'What a save!' Alisson screamed at the TV, just like his dad.

A few minutes later, Marcos was called into action again. He rushed out to dive bravely at Mbo Mpenza's feet.

'What a block!'

But Belgium kept on attacking. Wilmots dribbled into the Brazil box and curled a shot towards the top corner. Up jumped Marcos to complete his hat-trick of super saves.

'What a hero!'

Thanks to their incredible keeper, Brazil were still in the game, and eventually, Rivaldo and Ronaldo scored the goals to send them through to the quarter-finals.

'Marcos was definitely our man of the match!' Alisson announced at the final whistle. His brother nodded his head in agreement. Muriel was a keeper too, after all.

One thing was for certain – Brazil would have to play much better to beat their next opponents. England had an excellent team, featuring David Beckham in midfield and Michael Owen in attack. It was Owen who scored the opening goal, but Brazil bounced back thanks to two magical moments from Ronaldinho.

'Semi-finals, here we come!' Alisson and Muriel

celebrated like their heroes out on the pitch in Japan.

There was just so much to love about that Brazilian team:

The size and strength of centre-backs Lúcio and Edmílson,

The pace and power of wing-backs Cafu and Roberto Carlos,

The end-to-end energy of midfielders Gilberto Silva and Kléberson,

The skill and shooting of 'The Three Rs', Ronaldinho, Rivaldo and Ronaldo...

'And don't forget about marvellous Marcos!'

Together, Brazil were just too good for Turkey in the semi-finals, and were through to another World Cup final after winning 1–0! There, they faced another European giant: Germany.

'I can't watch! I can't watch!' José kept saying before kick-off, but of course he watched every single nervous minute with them.

'Come on, Brazil!'

Although they had lots of chances in the first

half, they failed to score any of them. And while it was still 0–0, Germany were still in the game...

Early in the second half, Brazil gave away a free kick a long way from their goal. It didn't look like a very dangerous position, but Oliver Neuville ran up and fired a ferocious shot towards the top corner.

'Noooo!' José groaned, fearing the worst, but Marcos flew through the air to tip it onto the post.

'What a save!' Alisson shouted admiringly.

That shock seemed to wake up Brazil's star attackers. They had a goal to score and a World Cup to win!

Rivaldo's shot was spilled by Oliver Kahn and Ronaldo was there for the rebound. *1–0!*

'Goooooaaaaaallllllll!!!!' Alisson didn't dunk his face in a cake like his dad had, but he did jump up and down on the sofa.

Ten minutes later, Rivaldo dummied Kléberson's pass, letting it run through to Ronaldo. *2–0!*

Game over – Brazil were the new World Champions! It was a night – and a tournament –

that proud young Alisson would never forget. As
he watched the players celebrating on the pitch, he
felt like he was looking into his own future.
Suddenly, it all seemed so clear. That was going to
be him one day – starring for Brazil, winning the
World Cup for his country.

CHAPTER 5

INTO THE YOUTH TEAM
AT INTERNACIONAL

After Brazil's triumph, Alisson had never felt so inspired, but he still had a long way to go before he could make his own World Cup dream come true. After all, he didn't even play for a proper, professional football club.

It was surely only a matter of time, though. Even in that first kickaround after Muriel's training session, the Internacional youth coach had spotted Alisson's talent. The boy was skilful enough with his feet to be a good outfield player, but in goal, he already had the technique to be truly *GREAT*.

'Goalkeeping must run in the family!' the coach thought to himself. He decided to speak to Alisson's

dad as soon as possible about signing him up for
the academy.

'You better watch out, bro,' Alisson joked with
Muriel, 'because soon *I'm* going to be the Number 1
around here!'

Confidence was important for a young footballer,
but so was the desire to improve. And Alisson was
eager to learn *EVERYTHING* about being an excellent
goalkeeper. He had been studying his heroes carefully
for ages – his dad, his brother, Taffarel, Marcos,
Germany's Oliver Kahn – but now it was time to put
all of that watching into practice on the pitch.

'Bring it on!' Alisson said to himself as he arrived
for his first session at Internacional. He was ready to
show his new coaches that Muriel wasn't the only
brilliant young Becker in town.

After a few warm-up kicks and catches, Alisson
couldn't wait to get started for real. Soon, the
Internacional outfield players were lining up to take
it in turns to pass and then shoot at goal, while
the Internacional keepers took it in turns to try to
save them.

As the new kid in the team, Alisson was determined to make a fantastic first impression. However many shots the other keepers saved, he had to save more!

Alisson was the last to take his turn in goal, and so far, every single player had scored. There had been a few unstoppable shots, straight into the top corner, but there had also been some pretty poor goalkeeping.

'Oooh, I reckon I could definitely have saved that!' Alisson had thought to himself as one of his rivals had allowed a ball to squirm under his diving body.

Now, it was time to prove it. As he took up his position on the goal line, he tightened the straps on his gloves and stared straight ahead with full focus.

He watched as Internacional's young star striker placed the ball down, passed it to the coach and then kept running forward, into the penalty area, to collect the one-two...

Alisson was off his line in a flash, rushing bravely towards the ball in classic, crazy Becker fashion.

...The striker had no choice but to shoot first time,

low and hard towards the bottom corner. *BANG!*
But Alisson spread out his arms and legs to make
himself as tall and wide as possible for the block.
SAVED!

As he got back up, Alisson was bursting with
pride. One shot, one save – it was exactly the
fantastic first impression that he had been hoping
for. The other keepers looked devastated, and so did
the star striker. His 100 per cent record was gone,
and he wasn't happy about it.

'Hey, that keeper cheated!' the striker protested
angrily. 'He came off his line.'

'And?' the Internacional coach replied with a
shrug of his shoulders. 'What's wrong with that? He
was just being clever – well done, keeper!'

Alisson was delighted to hear that praise, but he
tried not to show it. He just did a quick fist-pump
and then prepared himself for the next challenge:

Two shots, two saves,

Three shots, three saves...

In the end, Alisson did let one goal in, but he
wasn't too disappointed about that. It had taken a

beautiful strike to beat him, and by then, he had already made his fantastic first impression.

And he wasn't finished shining yet. During the match at the end, he calmly controlled a back-pass and then set up a goal for his team with a perfect long pass from inside his own penalty area.

Wow! The coaches looked at each other as if they couldn't believe what they had just seen, especially from a ten-year-old kid. His composure was amazing, and so was his kicking accuracy. Was Alisson going to be even better than his brother?

'Great work today,' the Internacional youth team manager said after the session, giving him a big pat on the back. 'Welcome to the team. Who knows, maybe we've got Internacional's Next Number 1 right here!'

Alisson just smiled shyly, but in his head, he added, 'And Brazil's!'

CHAPTER 6

BROTHERLY BATTLES AT HOME

Now that Alisson and Muriel were both playing for the Internacional academy – and in the same position too – their brotherly battles were even more competitive than ever. Especially at home, where the Beckers had just moved from their old apartment to a brand-new, bigger house.

Alisson and Muriel did miss playing football with their friends out in the streets every day and night, but now they could play 1 vs 1 inside their own home. It didn't take much effort or organisation. Once their parents were out, they just opened the living room doors and used them as goalposts. They played with a small plastic ball to cause less damage, but that didn't really make their brotherly battles any less daring or dangerous.

'Are you ready?'

'YEAH! Are you ready?'

'YEAH!'

'Right, let the battle begin!'

This 1 vs 1 game was an exciting new challenge for them both because they weren't just crazy keepers anymore. No, now they had to play every single position on the football pitch, all at the same time. One second, Alisson was dribbling forward on the attack, and the next he was sliding in for a tough tackle on Muriel, taking care not to knock over all the new, expensive furniture.

'Phew, that was close… PLAY ON!'

The speed was frantic, and the challenges were ferocious. With family pride on the line, their games sometimes looked more like war than football! But thanks to all those afternoons as a one-boy team, Alisson's all-round football skills were getting better and better. He had always been a pretty talented player, but now he was learning to twist and turn

in the tiniest spaces of their living room. Fancy
footwork was unusual for a keeper, but Alisson
wasn't interested in being an ordinary keeper, who
only used his hands. He wanted to be *extra*ordinary,
like Victor Valdés.

Valdés was Barcelona's next big keeper and he
was brilliant on the ball. The Spaniard loved to start
attacks with quick, short passes to his teammates.
And then when they were defending, he played like
a sweeper keeper, always ready to rush out of his
goal at the first sign of danger. That way, Valdés was
always involved in the game, even if Barcelona
were winning 4–0.

'That's my kind of keeper!' Alisson thought to
himself as he watched his new hero in action. He
wanted to be just like Valdés when he was older.

But the brotherly battles weren't just a great way
for Alisson to practise controlling the ball; they
were also a great way for him to practise controlling
his emotions. Although his brother was a lot bigger
and stronger, and still brilliant at winding him up, in
their 1 vs 1 games there was no referee. That meant

no fouls, no rules, and no-one to go crying to if things went wrong. So, no matter what Muriel said or did to him, Alisson had to try to just keep calm and carry on.

Most days, their aggressive brotherly battles went on and on and on, until one of them got hurt, or, more importantly, one of their parents came home.

'Quick – tidy up!' Muriel shouted to Alisson as soon as he heard the sound of the key in the front door. After a quick argument over the score – 3–2 to Muriel, they agreed eventually – they rushed around clearing up the mess they had made. They straightened the sofa cushions, put all the fragile items back where they belonged, and closed the living room doors again. Perfect!

As they looked around the room, they were pleased with their work. Everything was back to normal, as if nothing had ever happened. Their red, sweat-drenched faces were the only sign left that an important battle had just taken place.

'Hi boys, how are you doing?' their mum asked as they came over to help her with the shopping bags.

'Good, thanks!'

'What have you been up to this afternoon?'

'Oh, nothing much, mainly just sitting around watching TV,' the little liars told her, looking as innocent as could be.

But Magali couldn't be fooled that easily. No, she knew her football-mad sons too well to believe that rubbish.

'Really?' she laughed. 'Well, if watching TV makes you two that sweaty, maybe you need to do some extra fitness training!'

CHAPTER 7

TOO SMALL TO SAVE THE DAY?

Alisson's first few years at the Internacional academy flew by happily, filled with saves and clean sheets. He was getting better all the time, working his way towards his dream of being the greatest goalkeeper for his club and country,.

But at the age of thirteen, that all changed. Suddenly, Alisson wasn't his team's Number 1 anymore, or the second choice keeper either. It wasn't a question of skill, though; it was a question of size. Now that they were all teenagers, a lot of his teammates were growing taller and taller, especially the goalkeepers. Some of them could touch the crossbar without even jumping!

Alisson was in trouble. Height was so important for a goalkeeper. Everyone knew that the best shot-stoppers were always big and strong. If he didn't grow soon, he was going to be left behind on the bench forever.

'Why am I not getting taller like everyone else?' Alisson asked his parents miserably after yet another training session as the third-choice keeper. 'Muriel wasn't this small at my age!'

There was no simple answer to that, but his parents did their best to comfort him. 'Son, I know it's hard, but you've just got to be patient. Some kids mature early and some mature later. Everyone is different, but your growth spurt *will* come, we promise!'

While Alisson waited impatiently for that day to arrive, he focused on improving himself in other ways. After all, being a great goalkeeper wasn't all about height. It was also about technique, and he was still the best keeper in the squad for that. He could fly through the air to save shots that no-one else could, and his long passes were phenomenal.

It was also about bravery, and he was still the best keeper in the squad for that too. Alisson was brilliant at catching crosses, even in the most crowded penalty areas, and he was totally fearless in a 1 vs 1 situation. He would do anything to stop the other team from scoring.

It was also about fitness. Hmm, that was an area where Alisson definitely had lots of work to do. He had always loved unhealthy food – especially sweet snacks and fast food, and now that he'd lost his place in the team, he was eating more and more of them. That made him slower in the team warm-ups, and also slower off his goal line in games.

'Come on, you've got to be quicker to that ball, kid!' Daniel Pavan, the Internacional goalkeeper coach, called out to him.

'Sorry!' Alisson muttered as he trudged back to his goal. Even a short sprint to the edge of his penalty area felt more like a marathon these days. What was the point anymore?

It was a famous Internacional victory that helped to kick-start Alisson's incredible recovery. In 2006, the senior team made it all the way to the FIFA Club World Cup Final. It was already an amazing achievement, but their last opponents in the tournament would be a brilliant Barcelona team, starring Valdés, Carles Puyol, Deco, Andrés Iniesta and Ronaldinho.

Surely, it was all over for Internacional? But no, the team defended brilliantly and then, with time running out, they shocked Barcelona by scoring a late winning goal. *1–0!*

'Yes, yes, yes!' Alisson screamed, jumping off the sofa and dancing around the living room. He couldn't believe what he had just seen. What a win – he loved his local club more than ever now!

So Alisson decided that things had to change, starting with his diet. If he was still serious about being a professional footballer, it was time to get fit and healthy again. Otherwise, even a gigantic growth spurt wasn't going to save his goalkeeping career.

'Much better!' Pavan told him as he stood there panting heavily on the finish line.

Alisson was sweating even more than he did

during his brotherly battles with Muriel, but at least he was starting to feel faster and more energetic again.

'Excellent!' Pavan said as he raced out to beat the striker to the ball.

He allowed himself a little smile as he jogged back to his goal line. The old Alisson was back. All he had to do now was reclaim the Number 1 shirt and then become Internacional's hero in the Nike Cup. Hurray!

The Nike Cup was a big deal for all young footballers in Brazil, but especially for the Beckers. Alisson had been waiting a long time for his chance to finally come. He had been waiting six years to be exact, ever since Muriel had proudly returned from the Nike Cup with the Best Keeper prize.

Alisson could still remember the mix of joy and jealousy that he had felt that day. Every time he saw Muriel's trophy glistening on the shelf at home, he told himself, 'I want to win one of those too!' Now, six years on, his big moment was here. It was his turn to save the day for Internacional.

But sadly, his manager had a different idea. Despite all of his hard work in training, Alisson didn't play a single minute of a single match.

'What a waste of time!' he thought as he stood on the sidelines, with his shoulders slumped.

By the end of the day, Alisson was so humiliated and heartbroken that he was ready to give up on his football dream. If he was still the third-choice keeper in the Internacional academy, how was he ever going to become the first-choice keeper for Brazil and win the World Cup?

Other teenage hopefuls were flourishing. Iker Casillas had joined the Real Madrid senior squad at the age of sixteen, and Gianluigi Buffon had made his debut for Parma at the age of seventeen. Now aged fifteen, Alisson still felt a million miles away from the Internacional first team. What chance did he have of making it to the top, and was it really worth waiting around for? Maybe it was time for him to try a different sport. Maybe he would always be too small to save the day.

Alisson's parents were starting to think the same

too. They could see that their son's keeping career wasn't going well, and they were struggling to pay for all his kit and travel. Wouldn't it be better if Alisson stopped playing football and focused on his studies instead?

But luckily one man still believed in Alisson as Brazil's Future Number 1.

'Let him stay here a bit longer,' Pavan, the Internacional goalkeeping coach, persuaded José. 'I know things aren't going too well for him right now, but your son has a very special talent.'

CHAPTER 8

ONE MORE YEAR

'It would be a massive mistake for him to go now!'
Pavan argued. He had decided to speak to the other
coaches about Alisson, but he found that not many
of them agreed with him. 'He's got so much
potential. I really think that he's got all the skills
to be a great goalkeeper – catching, kicking, calm,
concentration, decision-making...'

'Yes, but the boy's too small – it's as simple as
that!'

'Well, we should at least wait to see if he grows.
He's not even sixteen yet!'

One more year – that's what the Internacional
academy decided eventually, after lots of discussion.

After that, if Alisson still hadn't grown any taller, sadly they would have to let him go.

Some young players might have seen that as a lot of pressure, but not Alisson. He was a much calmer character these days. Instead, he saw it as a challenge. He had twelve more months to show the club's youth coaches that he was just too good for them to give up on.

'A lot can change in a year,' Alisson said to Pavan with a very determined look on his face. He had plenty of work to do.

Alisson trained harder than ever to become the best goalkeeper he could be. It wasn't always fun, but that wasn't the point. This was his last chance to make his dream come true. So he practised everything over and over again until it was as perfect as possible:

Kicking the ball long,

Kicking the ball short,

Throwing the ball,

Rolling the ball,

Catching the ball,

55

Punching the ball,
Saving shots to his right,
Saving shots to his left,
Saving shots up high,
Saving shots down low,
Saving shots heading for the top corner,
Saving shots heading for the bottom corner...

The list went on and on. But with Pavan's help, Alisson was making big improvements in all areas of his game. He felt fitter, more focused and more confident as well.

And then one day, it finally happened – Alisson started to grow! And once he started, he just kept on growing:

One more centimetre, two more centimetres, three more centimetres... seventeen more centimetres!

'My little boy!' Magali gasped as her youngest son walked through the front door and towered over her. She would have to get used to that sight. 'I

know we always told you that your growth spurt
would come, but I didn't expect it to be so sudden!'

'Woah, you're taller than me now!' Muriel
declared as they stood back-to-back in front of the
mirror at home.

Alisson grinned. Not only was he taller than his big
brother, but he was also taller than Valdés, Casillas
and Taffarel, three of his ultimate football heroes. He
was already an impressive height for a goalkeeper,
and he was still growing.

'There's nothing stopping me now,' Alisson told
himself as he looked down at his huge hands.
Suddenly, he felt so powerful, like a superhero after
a turbo boost. All that extra training had been worth
it because now he had the size *and* the skill to
become Brazil's next great goalkeeper. What was
he waiting for?!

In no time, Alisson was back to being the
Number 1 again in the Internacional academy team.
After all, he was now the biggest keeper, as well
as the best. Thank goodness the coaches had
decided to give him one more year! And this time,

he was going to make sure that he held on tightly to that precious starting spot, as if it were a fiercely-hit football.

'Well, until the first team come calling for me, anyway!' he joked with Pavan. Now that he had achieved the first part of his plan, he was already looking ahead to his next challenge.

The Internacional goalkeeping coach was so pleased for his young protégé. He deserved his success after all his hard work.

Now, Alisson just needed to keep saving the day for the youth team, and hopefully, important people would be watching.

CHAPTER 9

BREAKTHROUGH WITH BRAZIL

Alisson always tried to be a calm character, both on and off the pitch. When he wasn't saving the day for Internacional, he loved relaxing at the beach with his friends – eating, laughing, lying in the sun, and of course, playing a bit of beach football in between.

'Before you ask – there's no way I'm going in goal!' Alisson told his friends with a smile as the game began. 'I do that all the time at Internacional. No, I'm going to be a striker today!'

Time flies when you're having fun playing football. Before Alisson knew it, hours had passed, and when he went over to check his phone, he had lots of missed calls from his grandad.

'Uh oh, something bad must have happened!' Alisson feared. His heart was hammering with dread as he called back.

'What's wrong, Grandad?'

'Nothing, but you've got to come home right now,' he replied, although he didn't sound very worried.

Really? Alisson was going to need more information than that before he stopped playing beach football with his friends. 'Why?'

He heard his grandad sigh. 'I wanted to wait until you got here, but okay, I'll tell you now. You've been called up to the Brazil Under-17s!'

What?! At first, Alisson didn't believe it. His first thought was, 'It must be a joke!' His grandad was always playing pranks on the family. But it did seem like a strange thing for him to make up…

'Okay, I'm on my way home now,' he told his grandad and then ended the call.

Seconds later, his phone was ringing again. This time, it was his uncle.

'Congratulations, kid! It's such great news that you've been called up to the national team.'

Alisson didn't know what to think anymore. Was his uncle telling the truth, or was he part of the prank too?

There was only one way to find out. Alisson raced home as fast as he could to check the official Brazil website. His hand was trembling with excitement as he clicked to see the latest Under-17 squad. And there it was, his name, first on the list:

ALISSON BECKER

Wow, it wasn't a joke; it was true! He really was going to represent his country at the 2009 Under-17 World Cup in Nigeria. What an honour!

'See?' his grandad grinned. 'I can't believe that you thought I'd trick you about something like that. Right, this calls for a family celebration!'

A few weeks later, Alisson was on his way to Nigeria, alongside twenty more of Brazil's best young footballers. They included a creative little midfielder called Philippe Coutinho and a wonderkid named Neymar Jr, who people were already calling 'The New Pelé'. After trying to stop him from scoring in training, Alisson was just glad that they were on the same national team.

'This is going to be so much fun,' he told Romário Leiria, who was also at the Internacional academy. 'We're going to win the World Cup!'

Sadly, that dream didn't come true. Despite all their talent, the Brazil players just couldn't find their best form together. They did beat Japan 3–2 in their first match, but that was thanks to Alisson's great goalkeeping and then a last-minute winner from Wellington Nem.

'Come on, we've got to do better than that!' their coach, Lucho Nizzo, urged them.

But in their second game, Brazil's brilliant attackers just couldn't find a way past the Mexico keeper, José Rodríguez. Alisson watched with frustration as his teammates missed chance after chance.

'Nooooo!' he groaned as Wellington somehow fired another easy shot wide.

Although most of the action was happening at the other end, Alisson kept his concentration well. He couldn't switch off, not when his country was counting on him to save the day. When Mexico attacked, he was ready to react. He stopped a shot from close range and then he punched a free kick away for a corner-kick.

'Focus!' Alisson shouted at his defenders, clapping his gloves together.

But it was Brazil's goalkeeper himself who forgot to focus. In the seventieth minute, Mexico curled a corner into the box. It should have been a simple catch for Alisson, but at the last second, the ball squirmed out of his gloves. And before he could make up for his mistake, Mexico had scored. *1–0!*

'Nooooo!' Alisson groaned, much louder this time.

After that shock defeat, it was Alisson who took most of the blame. That was the hardest part of being a goalkeeper. He had made lots of good saves during the game, but of course, it was his one mistake that everyone was talking about.

'What a disaster! What was the keeper doing there?'

'He's got to catch that – there's no excuse for that error!'

The criticism hurt, but Alisson was strong enough

to bounce back. He was still young and still learning at the top level. Plus, Brazil's World Cup wasn't over yet. With a win over Switzerland, they could still make it through to the Round of 16.

'Come on, let's do this!' Alisson cheered in the tunnel before kick-off.

With the pressure on, Brazil started brilliantly. Philippe and Neymar Jr were linking up beautifully and looking really dangerous together. There was only one, very important thing missing: a goal. Until they scored, Switzerland were still in the game.

In the twentieth minute, they won a corner. Granit Xhaka curled the ball towards the Brazilian back post, where Pajtim Kasami jumped highest to head it goalwards. Surely, he would score...

But in a flash, Alisson threw himself to the ground and made a super save to keep the ball out. Brilliant! Unfortunately, however, he couldn't get back up in time to stop a Swiss player from heading home the rebound. *1–0!*

'Keep going!' Nizzo called out on the touchline. 'There's still lots of time left!'

But it was like the Mexico match all over again. As hard as Philippe and Neymar Jr tried, they just couldn't get the ball in the net. At the final whistle, the Brazilians collapsed on the grass in disbelief. Was their World Cup really over, already?

On the long journey home, Alisson was disappointed but not distraught. Apart from that one mistake against Mexico, he had played well, making some memorable saves. He could hold his head up high, and hopefully, he would have more chances to bring back a trophy for Brazil.

CHAPTER 10

BROTHERLY BATTLES AT INTERNACIONAL

At the end of his Under-17 World Cup experience, Alisson returned to Internacional, ready to carry on working his way up towards the first team. He had learnt a lot during the tournament, but just because he was a Brazilian youth international now, it didn't mean that he could walk into his club's senior squad straight away. No, he knew that he would need to stay calm and patient, and take things one step at a time.

Under-18s, Under-20s, Under-23s...

After all, Internacional already had some very good goalkeepers:

Lauro,

Renan,

Agenor Detofol,

and, of course, Muriel.

Yes, while Alisson was busy breaking into the Internacional Under-20s, his big brother was getting closer and closer to becoming the club's first-choice keeper. In 2011, Muriel at last achieved his aim; he was starting most league matches in front of thousands of fans at the Beira Rio Stadium.

'Honestly, it's the best feeling ever,' he babbled excitedly. 'I don't even know how to describe it!'

As he listened, Alisson felt a mixture of joy and jealousy, just like when Muriel had won the Best Keeper award at the Nike Cup. Of course he was pleased for his elder brother, but at the same time, he couldn't help wishing that it was him playing in goal for Internacional.

'One day,' he told himself, once again using Muriel's success as an extra motivation.

When the Internacional Under-20s made it through to the Championship semi-finals, Alisson

was their back-up keeper. But after weeks of
waiting impatiently for a chance to play, suddenly
he was called into action against their local rivals
Grêmio.

'Good luck!' Rafael Copetti, the first-choice
keeper, said to him as he came off halfway through
the game.

This was it – Alisson's big, breakthrough moment.
Could he step up and save the day for Inter? It was
never easy for a keeper coming on in the middle of
a match. He wasn't properly warmed up as he ran
onto the field, but his head was definitely in the
game. He was determined to be the hero.

Alisson played well under pressure, and there
was nothing he could do to stop Everton Júnior's
equaliser. At the final whistle, it was Internacional 1
Grêmio 1. Time for penalties!

As he took up his position on the goal line,
Alisson thought of his idol, Taffarel, and his save
against the Netherlands in the 1998 World Cup
semi-final shoot-out. Could he do something similar
now for Internacional? His team needed him!

Alisson couldn't keep out Grêmio's first spot-kick, but he dived the right way for the second. With a strong arm, he pushed the ball away. *Saved!*

'Come on!' Alisson roared, punching the air with passion.

A few penalties later, Internacional were the winners. They were through to the final, thanks to their brilliant back-up keeper.

With heroics like that, it wasn't long before Alisson was breaking into the Under-23s team. At first, the fans wondered, 'Is he going to be as good as his brother?' But many amazing saves later, they were asking a slightly different question:

'Is Alisson going to be *better* than Muriel?'

Their brotherly battle was back on, and this time it wasn't taking place in the living room at home. No, now every day at first-team training, they were fighting to be Internacional's first-choice keeper.

'May the best player win,' they agreed.

Although they were football rivals, Alisson and Muriel still had lots of love and respect for each other. They were family – a family of crazy keepers.

So instead of trying to trip each other up, they pushed each other to perform better.

'Come on old man, twenty more minutes!'

'Are you tired already, bro? This is just the beginning!'

The Becker brothers were determined to make it to the top together.

And their plan was working perfectly. After impressing the manager, Dunga, in practice, Alisson got to play his first senior game for Internacional in the local championship against Cruzeiro.

On his big debut, Alisson looked unbeatable. In the first half, he made two super saves and early in the second, he rushed out bravely to beat the striker to the ball.

'Great work, keeper!' the Internacional fans cheered.

But just when Alisson allowed himself to think about a first clean sheet, Cruzeiro attacked again and this time, they scored with an unstoppable strike. *1–1!*

When the final whistle blew, Alisson was a bit

disappointed with the draw, but Dunga was full of praise. 'Well played. You really saved us today. If it wasn't for you, we would have lost that.'

With those words in his ears, Alisson couldn't wait for his next chance to shine.

At the start of the 2013 Brazilian League season, Muriel wore the Number 1 shirt, Agenor was the reserve and Alisson was third choice. However, it didn't stay that way for long. Soon, Alisson had skipped ahead of Agenor to become his brother's back-up. And after only six games on the bench, he was lucky enough to slide into the starting line-up!

'Good luck, bro,' Muriel said, despite feeling frustrated about losing his place in the team.

'Thanks, you'll be back in no time!'

Wow – it was a massive moment for Alisson, in front of a huge home crowd, but he was confident that he could handle the pressure. That's what being a great goalkeeper was all about.

'You'll be brilliant,' Internacional's experienced striker, Diego Forlán, reassured him before kick-off.

'And we'll try to make sure that you don't have very much to do anyway!'

Alisson was feeling hopeful when Andrés D'Alessandro scored in the first half, but their opponents Goiás soon fought back. With the rain falling heavily, Renan Oliveira broke through the Internacional defence and slid a splashing shot past Alisson's outstretched leg. *1–1!*

After that, the goals kept coming, just like the rain.

Alisson skidded across the muddy goalmouth to stop a header, but Goiás still managed to score off the rebound. *2–1!*

'Offside!' Alisson yelled at the linesman, but the flag stayed down.

His difficult Brazilian League debut continued. Four minutes later, Ramón ran into the box and steered his header past Alisson's desperate dive. *3–1!*

'This is a disaster!' Alisson thought to himself as he threw the ball angrily towards the halfway line. Conceding three goals was never a fun feeling, even if they hadn't been his fault.

Fortunately, the game wasn't finished yet,

though, and neither were Internacional. With two goals in eight minutes, they managed to equalise.

What a crazy game: 3–3! Alisson was relieved about the final result, but he couldn't help worrying. What if he was dropped from the team after only one match?

But no, Dunga believed in him, and in his next two appearances, Alisson collected two clean sheets.

'That's more like it!' he cheered after an excellent 1–0 win against Corinthians. His confidence was growing with every game, and he could tell that the defenders were starting to trust him.

So, was Alisson now Internacional's new Number 1? No, not quite yet. First, he would need to become a more consistent keeper. That would take time and experience. When he made two mistakes in two matches, Dunga decided to bring Muriel back into the team, swapping one Becker brother for the other.

Alisson wasn't happy about losing his starting spot, but he stayed calm and carried on training hard. He knew what he had to work on, and after that first taste of first-team football, he wanted more of it. Lots more of it.

'Whatever it takes, I'm going to make that Number 1 shirt mine!' Alisson declared, his eyes burning brightly with ambition.

CHAPTER 11

TOULON TRIUMPH

Alisson's next exciting international adventure was
to France to play in the 2013 Toulon Tournament.
It was one of the biggest youth competitions in the
world, but his beloved Brazil hadn't won it since
2002.

That year, their team had featured future
superstars Dani Alves, Diego and Adriano. So, what
about the team of 2013? Well, there was no Philippe
and no Neymar Jr either, but Brazil still had plenty of
talented players, and of course, a great goalkeeper.

At twenty, Alisson was one of the oldest players
in the squad, and so he felt like a leader. Centre-
back Dória wore the captain's armband, but really,

it was a big team effort. Brazil were in Group B
with Belgium, Portugal, Nigeria, and Alisson's old
rivals, Mexico. It wasn't going to be easy, but if they
all worked together, they believed that they could
beat anyone.

'Come on, let's lift that trophy!' Alisson announced
ahead of the first game against Belgium.

He was fired up and ready to shine. He knew that
a successful Toulon Tournament could help turn a
talented young player like him into a future superstar.
Dani Alves, Alan Shearer, Thierry Henry, Javier
Mascherano, even French goalkeeper Hugo Lloris – it
had happened to all of them. So why couldn't Alisson
be next? There would be lots of scouts watching
from all over the world, and if he performed well,
he could make a real name for himself. Then
Internacional might give him the Number 1 shirt
and who knew, maybe the Brazil senior team would
come calling...

However, Alisson's tournament started in the
worst possible way. After thirteen minutes against
Belgium, Brazil were 1–0 down and it was all

Alisson's fault. Igor Vetokele's shot came straight at him, but somehow, he spilled the ball into his own net.

'Noooooo!' Alisson groaned as he turned to see it trickle over the goal line.

Oh dear, was this going to be the Under-17 World Cup all over again? No, because this time Brazil were stronger and smarter than before, and they showed it by fighting back to win 2–1. Phew!

'Sorry about my mistake,' a relieved Alisson told his teammates after the game. 'It won't happen again, I promise!'

And he kept that promise in the games that followed.

Brazil 1 Mexico 0

They had beaten the defending champions! For Alisson, it felt like sweet revenge. This time, he kept his concentration, from the first minute until the last. He showed that he had the safest hands around.

Brazil 2 Portugal 0

Even when the game was already won, Alisson stayed alert in his penalty area, ready to deal with any sudden signs of danger. He wasn't letting any more goals in – no way.

'Come on!' he cheered at the final whistle, celebrating another clean sheet.

When the coach took Alisson off at half-time against Nigeria, Brazil were winning 1–0. But without their great goalkeeper, they could only draw 1–1.

'Don't worry, I'll be back for the final!' Alisson reassured everyone. It felt good to know that his country was counting on him.

Yes, Brazil were now just one game away from glory. As the winners of Group B, they were up against the winners of Group A, Colombia. It was going to be a fierce South American clash in the south of France. And Alisson couldn't wait.

Having started badly in their first match, Brazil began the final in terrific form. From an early corner, Vinícius Araújo somehow managed to bundle the ball into the net. *1–0!*

'Yes!' Alisson shouted, punching the air on the edge of his penalty area. It wasn't the classic, beautiful kind of football that Brazil was renowned

for, but who cared about that? A goal was a goal –
they all counted.

And now, Alisson's hard work began. He tightened
his glove straps and focused his mind. He was going
to do everything he could to protect their lead. He
wasn't letting any more goals in – no way.

Along with the captain Dória, Alisson organised
the defence in front of him, telling them where to be
and who to mark. The Brazilian backline had been
so strong all tournament, and now, they just needed
one last push.

'Well done, guys – keep going!' he encouraged
them.

In the second half, Alisson was called into action.
A Colombia free kick curled around the wall and
dipped down towards the bottom corner. But Brazil's
Number 1 flew across his goal and pushed the ball
away from danger. It was going to take a very special
shot to get past Alisson's safe hands.

At the final whistle, Alisson threw his arms up
triumphantly. They had done it – Brazil were the
winners of the Toulon Tournament. What a brilliant

team effort! The Brazil players ran around the pitch hugging and high-fiving each other. It was time to get the Samba celebrations started.

'*Campeones, Campeones, Olé! Olé! Olé!*' Alisson sang, jumping up and down as his teammates danced around him.

Alisson hadn't had that many saves to make in goal, but when his nation needed him, he had always been there to save the day. He felt so proud to be a part of such a united group of players. Brazil were usually famous for their attacking flair, not their defensive force, but this team was different. They had worked so hard to only concede two goals in five games. That was an amazing achievement.

Sadly, Alisson didn't win the tournament's Best Keeper award, but he didn't mind that, just as long as he had his winner's medal and a gloved hand on the trophy.

'Hurray!' the Brazilians cheered, holding it up high together as a team.

CHAPTER 12

LEARNING FROM A WORLD CUP WINNER

After winning the Toulon tournament with Brazil, Alisson was feeling positive about the future. At the age of twenty, his football career was certainly moving in the right direction – towards the top! Now, it was time to grab hold of that Internacional Number 1 shirt and not let go.

'This is going to be my breakthrough year!' Alisson told himself as he prepared for the new league season.

There was a new challenge waiting for him, however. At Internacional, the competition amongst the keepers had just become even fiercer. Because as well as Muriel and Agenor, the club had also just signed a World Cup-winning goalkeeper. Dida was forty years old and coming to the end of his career, but he was still a big name with a big reputation in Brazil. Not only had he won the 2002 World Cup with the national team, but he had also lifted the Champions League trophy twice with Italian side AC Milan. He was a legend and he hadn't signed for Internacional to just sit on the bench. No, Dida expected to start every single game.

And at first, he did. During the early months of the season, Dida was the first-choice keeper and the other three took it in turns to be his back-up. It was frustrating for them all, but especially for the youngest.

'I don't want to wait another year to play,' Alisson complained to Muriel. 'I'm ready NOW!'

But what choice did he have? All he could do was stay patient, keep practising and try to learn as much as possible from working with a World Cup winner.

Fortunately, Dida was very happy to help his fellow keepers. With all his experience at major tournaments and in Europe, he had lots of useful tips to pass on.

'My main advice is do whatever it takes to stay
focused,' he told Alisson as they warmed up together
in training. 'Even if the ball is at the other end of the
pitch, you can still be involved. Remember, you're
part of the team too! Organise your defence, watch
the strikers, check your position, get ready to play a
pass. That way, you keep your head in the game and
your teammates will trust you more.'

'Thanks!'

Dida liked Alisson and he could see his star quality
straight away. He could tell that Alisson was much
more than just an excellent shot-stopper; he had
great understanding for the game and made very
wise decisions for a keeper so young. It wasn't easy
knowing when to rush out and when to stay in your
box, but Alisson had already mastered that difficult
skill. He was very comfortable on the ball too, even
when a striker was charging towards him at full speed.

'Wow, would you try that in a real match?' Dida
asked when Alisson fooled Andrés with a cheeky
Cruyff Turn in training.

He smiled and answered immediately. 'Of course!'

The thing that impressed Dida most about Alisson was his calm confidence. He moved around his penalty area in a way that said, 'Don't worry, I've got this!'

'And that's why you're going to be a top keeper,' Dida told him, with great certainty.

*

Away at Chapecoense, Alisson watched from the bench as Internacional's day just kept getting worse. They were already 4–0 down when Dida raced off his line and fouled the opposition striker.

Penalty! Red card!

Internacional had already made all of their substitutions, so sadly Alisson couldn't come on and save the day. But the game was already over, anyway. In his head, Alisson was already thinking ahead to their next match. With their Number 1 now suspended, the team would be needing their second keeper.

'This is your chance, kid,' Dida told him. 'Make the most of it!'

Alisson would do just that. There were eleven games left in the season and he started every single one.

At home against Fluminense, Fred's header was flying straight into the top corner, but somehow Alisson stretched his long arm out and kept it out. *SUPERSAVE!*

The danger wasn't over yet, though. The ball bounced out to Darío Conca, but Alisson sprang back up to block his shot too. *DOUBLE SUPERSAVE!*

As the Internacional fans chanted his name, Alisson calmly carried on being a great goalkeeper. He was just doing what he'd been born to do. He jumped high to tip shots over the bar, and he dived low to block balls heading for the bottom corner.

'I knew he was going to be great,' Dida thought to himself as he watched on from the bench.

Alisson did anything he could to stop his opponents from scoring. Against São Paulo, he blocked the first strike with his chest and the second with his face.

Paulão came over to check on his brave keeper

once the ball had been cleared. 'Are you okay?' he asked with concern.

'Of course, keep playing!' Alisson replied. He was back up on his feet, and fully focused on the game again.

With one game to go, Internacional were in fourth place in the Brazilian League. If they could win their final match, they would qualify for the Copa Libertadores, the biggest club competition in South America.

'Come on, we can do this!' the players cheered together before kick-off.

But away at Figueirense, the atmosphere was tense, and the Internacional team looked nervous. Luckily, Alisson was there to keep them calm and keep them in the game.

As the cross came towards him, the Figueirense striker was sure that he would score. But in a flash, Alisson threw himself down to make the save.

'Thanks!' Paulão said, high-fiving his incredible keeper.

A few minutes later, Alisson was at it again. As the

Figueirense winger dribbled towards him, he stood his ground, making himself look as tall and wide as possible. *BANG!* The shot was going in until Alisson stretched out his strong left arm to push it wide.

This time it was the other centre-back, Alan Costa, who came over to thank him. 'Phew, you really saved me there!'

But despite Alisson's dazzling display of saves, Internacional were still losing 1–0, with less than ten minutes to go. Were their Copa Libertadores dreams over?

No! Rafael Moura equalised and then in the very last minute of the match, Wellington Silva scored the winner. *2–1!*

So Internacional would be playing in the Copa Libertadores next season after all, and they had their great young goalkeeper to thank for that. At last, Alisson was the Number One now, and he was there to stay.

CHAPTER 13

INTER'S SPOT-KICK KING

In the quarter-finals of the 2015 Brazilian Cup, Alisson was having another amazing game in goal for Internacional.

As soon as his defenders gave the ball away near the centre circle, he was alert to the danger. However, he didn't rush out of his area like a crazy keeper. No, he was too calm and clever for that. Instead, he watched and waited until the time was right.

The Palmeiras striker dribbled forward and passed to his partner, but still Alisson waited behind his six-yard line. It was only when the Palmeiras striker got the ball back, just inside the box, that Alisson sprang into action. In a flash, he sprinted off his line and dived bravely at the striker's feet. *Saved!*

The Internacional fans in the stadium rose to their feet and roared. What would they do without their incredible new keeper?

A minute later, the Inter right-back Ernando went to clear the ball, but he kicked the winger instead. *Penalty to Palmeiras!*

'No way, ref!' Alisson protested at first, but he soon let go of his anger. What was done was done. Now he needed to stay calm and save his team yet again.

Taffarel, Dida… and now Alisson. He was making a name for himself as Brazil's next great spot-kick king. He had already stopped two penalties that season – one to win a shoot-out in the local championship and then one in the Copa Libertadores.

In their first year back in South America's biggest club competition, Internacional had made it all the way to the semi-finals. There, they faced the Mexican champions, Tigres. After winning the home leg in Brazil, they had high hopes of reaching the final, but in the second leg, Tigres taught them a harsh lesson. By half-time, Internacional were already 2–0 down, and early in the second half, they gave away a penalty. Uh oh, was this going to get embarrassing?

But no, Alisson had won his battle with the Tigres penalty taker, Rafael Sóbis. Not only had he guessed the right way, but he had also held onto the ball to stop any chance of a rebound.

'Come on!' Alisson called out, raising his arms like a true hero. As he launched an attack with an accurate long throw, he hoped that his supersave would inspire his team to victory.

Unfortunately, Internacional had lost that Copa Libertadores semi-final, but they were still in this Brazilian Cup quarter-final against Palmeiras, as long as their spot-kick king could save the day once more...

On his goal line, Alisson took a deep breath and clapped his gloves together. 'I can do this!' he told himself, focusing on the ball on the spot. 'I've done it many times before.'

It wasn't just luck that he was good at saving penalties. No, it was thanks to hours of hard work and preparation.

'That's it – don't dive too early,' Pavan told Alisson as they practised penalty after penalty. That was the key tactic. 'Wait until the last moment to make your move.'

But how was the goalie meant to guess the right way? Well, before every match, Alisson and Pavan sat and watched videos of the opponent's penalty taker together. Which side did he usually shoot? Did he prefer to go high or low? Was there a giveaway sign about which way he would go?

Alisson was also lucky to have Brazil's other spot-kick kings around to offer him lots of advice. Dida was still Internacional's reserve keeper and Taffarel was a club legend who was often there at training. They were both great examples for him to follow and learn from.

I can do this, I can do this!

As the Palmeiras striker Lucas Barrios started his run-up, Alisson threw his arms out wide to cover as much of the goal as he could. Then he bounced from foot to foot, getting ready to leap at the last moment.

Just before Barrios's boot struck the ball, Alisson made his move. He dived low to his right, but wait, the penalty was going higher and down the middle. No problem! He was agile enough to stretch up his strong left arm and stop the shot anyway. *Saved again!*

Once the ball had been cleared for a corner, the Internacional players ran over to congratulate their spot-kick king. Alisson was there at the centre of the crowd, thumping his chest with pride and passion.

'Come on!' he roared as Paulão jumped into his arms.

Just as Alisson hoped, that save sparked Internacional into life. Inspired by their great goalkeeper, they pushed forward on the attack and Alex scored a screamer. *1–0!*

Alisson punched the air with joy, but his dramatic day wasn't done yet. He made save after save to deny Palmeiras, until eventually, Rafael Marques beat him with a bullet header. *1–1!*

'Who was marking him?' Alisson exploded with anger. He was furious with his defence for letting him down. They had been so close to collecting another clean sheet.

Although he was disappointed with the draw, Alisson was very pleased with his own performance. And so was a very important person in the Beira-Rio crowd.

Dunga had coached Alisson at Internacional in the past, but now he was the manager of the Brazil national team. He left the stadium that night with a big smile on his face.

'Fantastic, I think I've found our new Number 1!'

CHAPTER 14

BRAZIL'S NEW NUMBER 1

The Brazilian team faced a big year in 2015. It had to be big, after their humiliating defeat to Germany in the 2014 World Cup semi-final: 7–1! And in front of a huge home crowd too – what a devastating day for the *Seleção!*

It was time for some serious changes. Straight after the tournament, Dunga had replaced Luiz Felipe Scolari as the Brazil manager, and started building a brand-new team.

New strikers,

New midfielders,

New defenders,

and, excitingly for Alisson, new goalkeepers!

Júlio César had been Brazil's Number 1 at the 2014 World Cup, but now, that role was up for grabs.

'I'm going to make it mine!' Alisson promised himself. That was his dream, and if he kept impressing at Internacional, why not? Anything could happen.

At first, Dunga gave the shirt to Jefferson, an experienced keeper who played for Botafogo. The brand-new Brazil got off to a good start, but in June 2015, they were beaten by Paraguay in the Copa América quarter-finals. Then three months later, when playing Chile in the qualifiers for the 2018 World Cup, a distracted Jefferson let the ball slip straight through his gloves, conceding a crucial goal. What a disaster!

'This isn't working,' Dunga told his goalkeeping coach afterwards. Brazil needed a safer pair of hands to protect their goal. 'Should we try someone else?'

There was Marcelo Grohe at Grêmio, or Diego Alves at Valencia. But Brazil's goalkeeping coach was... Taffarel! And he had an idea.

He nodded his head confidently. 'Don't worry, Dunga – I've got just the guy!'

Taffarel had been watching Alisson for years, and he knew that he was ready for the responsibility. He had proved that at Internacional in the Copa Libertadores. Yes, he was still only twenty-three years old, but so what? Talent was much more important than age or experience. Taffarel realised that Alisson reminded him a lot of himself – a calm, clever keeper who didn't make many mistakes – except he was even bigger and even better. Wasn't that exactly what the national team needed?

Some supporters, however, still weren't sure:

'Alisson? Is he really ready for this?'

'No way, it's too soon – he's just a kid!'

But Dunga didn't have any doubts, not after seeing Alisson's amazing performance against Palmeiras. So, for their next World Cup qualifier against Venezuela in October 2015, Brazil would have a brand-new goalkeeper.

'Congratulations, son!' Alisson's parents cried out when they heard the brilliant news.

'Nice one, bro!' Muriel added. 'Just don't mess this up, okay?'

Alisson was lost for words. Was he really going to start in goal for his beloved Brazil, the most successful national team in the world? Wow, what an honour! He really hadn't expected to get the call-up so soon. In his mind, he had been planning to play for the Under-23s at the 2016 Olympics, and then, hopefully if that went well, he would move up to the senior squad just in time for the 2018 World Cup.

But now, it was all happening a whole lot faster than that. Alisson was only moments away from walking out onto the pitch alongside international superstars like Dani Alves, Willian, Oscar and Kaká.

'Oh boy, this is big!'

As the match kicked off, Alisson did his best to stay calm and focused. 'This is just another, normal game,' he tried to tell himself, but of course, it wasn't. It was a game that would hopefully change his whole life completely.

Brazil's new Number 1 – that's what Alisson was aiming to become. He had worked so hard to get here, and he was determined to make the most of this massive opportunity. As his brother had said, he *couldn't* mess this up.

Just forty seconds later, Brazil were winning 1–0 thanks to a wonderstrike from Willian. Watching from his goal, Alisson allowed himself to relax just a tiny bit. Phew!

Alisson's first task of the game was to tip a Venezuela free kick around the post. It was a comfortable save but it also gave him that extra confidence boost he needed. As he got back up to his feet, he was already organising his defence for the corner-kick.

'Right, who's on the front post? Marquinhos, stick with your man!'

Alisson wasn't going to do things differently, just because it was his international debut. No, he was desperate to keep a clean sheet and impress his coach. He had to prove to Dunga that he could handle the pressure; in fact, it only made him stronger.

Other than some simple catches, Alisson didn't

have that much to do in the first half, but he kept moving around his penalty area and communicating with his teammates, just like Dida had taught him to do. He wasn't going to switch off, not even for a second.

Sadly, however, the Brazilian defence did switch off. In the second half, they left Christian Santos totally unmarked at the back post. Alisson rushed across his goal to get there, but there was nothing that he could do to stop Venezuela from scoring. *2–1 to Brazil!*

One little lapse in concentration and his dream clean sheet was gone.

'Come on, who was meant to be marking him?' Alisson screamed, waving his arms in frustration. 'That's not good enough, guys!'

Watching from the sidelines, Dunga wasn't happy with his team's defending, but he was delighted with his new Number 1. Even in his first game, Alisson was already showing signs of becoming a very important player for Brazil.

After starring in the next four World Cup qualifiers

in a row, Alisson felt settled in the starting line-up. He even collected his first clean sheet, against Peru. Everyone seemed to trust him now – the fans, Dunga *and* the defence. That was a good thing because it was time for him to play in his first senior international tournament: the Copa América. Brazil had been crowned the Champions of South America eight times before, but not since 2007. Now, in 2016, the pressure was on for them to lift the trophy once more.

'We can do this!' Alisson thought positively as the squad arrived in the USA. He still remembered his Toulon Tournament triumph from a few years earlier, and he wanted that glorious feeling again.

A goalless draw against Ecuador wasn't a good start, but things looked better after a 7–1 thrashing of Haiti. Now, all Brazil had to do was beat Peru, and they would be through to the quarter-finals.

'Let's go!' Their captain Dani Alves clapped and cheered.

As hard as they tried, however, Brazil just could not get the ball to go in. They created chance after chance, but every shot flew just over the bar, or was blocked by a brave defender.

'Keep going!' Alisson called out, keeping his concentration in goal.

As his teammates grew more and more frustrated, Peru pushed forward on the counter-attack. All of a sudden, Andy Polo raced away down the right wing. His cross flew past Alisson and then bounced off Raúl Ruidíaz and into the back of the net. *1–0!*

'But wait!' Alisson rushed straight over to the referee, pointing urgently at his arm. 'Hey, that's a handball!'

He was sure of it. He had seen the ball strike the Peruvian's arm, but unfortunately, the referee hadn't. *1–0 to Peru!*

Alisson couldn't believe it. Brazil were out of the Copa América and all because of a goal that shouldn't have been given. Football could be so unfair and cruel sometimes.

CHAPTER 15

INTEREST FROM ITALY

Despite Brazil's disappointing performance in 2016's Copa América, becoming Brazil's new Number 1 had changed Alisson's life completely. Suddenly, everyone was talking about him, even clubs in other countries.

'Really?' he asked his agent in disbelief. He repeated the sentence just to make sure that he had heard it right. 'Roma want to sign me?'

Alisson was very excited about the interest from Italy. Serie A was one of the most famous football leagues in the world. Taffarel had played for Parma and Dida for AC Milan.

'You should go, you'd love it there!' they both urged him.

Roma were a very good team, with lots of history, and they would be playing in the Champions League again next season. They had lots of top-quality players – Edin Džeko, Daniele De Rossi, Radja Nainggolan, Mohamed Salah, Francesco Totti... the list went on and on. Plus, there was a group of fellow Brazilians in the squad, including Bruno Peres at right-back and Juan Jesus at left-back.

'You could help make it a real Brazilian back-line!' Muriel joked.

That would certainly help him to feel more at home... Moving to Roma was a very tempting idea, but was Alisson really ready to leave Internacional, his local team, the club that he had played for since the age of ten? Although he had helped them win four local championships, there was still so much more for him to achieve – the Brazilian League title, the Copa Libertadores...

'You can always come back at the end of your career to do all that,' his parents suggested.

Okay, but what about all of Alisson's family and friends? Could he really leave them behind in Brazil?

'Don't worry, I've always wanted to visit Rome,' Muriel said with a smile, 'and now, I'll have somewhere to stay!'

In the end, Alisson decided that this was an opportunity that he couldn't waste. If he wanted to become the greatest goalkeeper in the world, then he needed to test himself against the greatest strikers in the world.

Lionel Messi, Cristiano Ronaldo, Luis Suárez, Sergio Agüero, Robert Lewandowski, Zlatan Ibrahimović – they were all playing in Europe. Even his old friend Neymar Jr was there now.

So, after one last clean sheet in the opening game of the 2016 Brazilian League season, Alisson waved goodbye to everyone at Internacional. He would miss them a lot, and one day he would be back. But for now, he was on his way to Italy, for £7 million.

'*Benvenuti a Roma!*' said the banners when he arrived.

Wearing a red club baseball cap and a yellow club scarf, Alisson posed for photos outside the Stadio Olimpico. It was the start of a big new adventure for him, and he felt both nervous and excited.

'Have I made the right decision?' Alisson asked himself as he tried to adapt to his new home. Everything was different now – the city, the country, the language, *and* the football club. It was like he was starting all over again. He would have to get to know all of his new teammates and prove to them that they could trust him to save the day. That would take time and lots of hard work on the training ground.

But what if it didn't work? What if they didn't like him? What if he wasn't as good as the other goalkeepers at the club? Bogdan Lobonț had been Roma's back-up keeper for years, while Wojciech Szczęsny was on loan from English giants Arsenal.

Though they were all friendly to each other in training, in truth they were rivals, competing for the starting spot. Bogdan was Number 18, and Alisson was Number 19. He had another big battle on his hands if he wanted to take the Number 1 spot from Wojciech.

It was in August 2016, during the Champions

League qualifiers, when Alisson got his first chance to shine. Roma's manager Luciano Spalletti decided to leave Wojciech on the bench for the team's trip to Porto.

'Right, I've got to make the most of this!' Alisson told himself as he warmed up in front of the fans. It was the last match before the Italian league season began, and so the manager would be making some big decisions about his line-up.

Alisson was desperate to impress, especially as he was up against one of his ultimate football heroes, the former Real Madrid keeper, Iker Casillas. Wow – as a youngster in the Internacional academy, he had looked up to the Spanish legend, and now he was sharing a pitch with him!

'Just act cool,' he told himself as they shook hands before kick-off.

Usually, with the pressure on, Alisson played better than ever, but this time, things didn't go quite so well. Sadly, it wasn't the dream Champions League debut that he'd been hoping for.

When a back-pass came to him, he kicked the ball

straight to a Porto attacker. Luckily, his shot flew high over the bar.

'Sorry!' Alisson called out, raising his hand. What was that? He was supposed to be good with the ball at his feet!

When Héctor Herrera hit a tame shot at goal, he dived down to save it, but it bounced straight back out to a Porto player. Luckily, the second strike went high and wide again.

'Focus!' Alisson shouted, to his teammates but also to himself. He was better than that. He was supposed to be one of the best shot-stoppers in the business!

And when Porto won a penalty, he guessed the right way, but he couldn't quite reach André Silva's powerful shot.

'So close!' Alisson groaned as he got back up to his feet. Although it had been a perfect penalty, he was still upset that he hadn't saved the day for his team. It felt like a wasted opportunity. He was supposed to be a spot-kick king!

The game ended in a 1–1 draw, which meant that Roma had an important away goal to take back to Italy. So it wasn't all doom and gloom, despite Alisson's disappointment.

'Hey, you played well,' Juan Jesus told him at the final whistle, trying to lift his spirits.

But Alisson still felt like he'd blown his big chance. When the second leg came around, he found himself on the bench. And with Wojciech in goal instead, Roma lost it 3–0.

Oh well, he told himself, they would be playing in the Europa League instead.

CHAPTER 16

ROMA'S NUMBER 2?

Most football clubs have one clear first-choice keeper, but during the 2016–17 season, Roma switched between two. Wojciech was their Number 1 in Serie A, while Alisson played in the two cup competitions: the Coppa Italia and the Europa League.

'It's good for you to have some healthy competition!' Spalletti told his keepers.

So, did that mean Alisson was Roma's second choice keeper? It was a strange situation, but at least he wasn't sitting on the bench every week. Luckily, he was getting lots of game-time in the Europa League, in which Roma finished top of their group. They didn't lose any of their group matches, although

they drew in their opening game, away to Viktoria
Plzeň, and after letting in one goal, Alisson knew that
if he wanted to become Roma's only Number 1,
he really had to prove himself on the pitch. That
meant keeping his concentration and keeping
clean sheets.

'No more mistakes!' he told himself.

The more matches he played, the more
comfortable Alisson felt in the team. It helped that
he had a strong and settled defence in front of him
– Federico Fazio and Kostas Manolas in the middle,
with the Brazilians Bruno and Juan on either side.
They trusted each other, and they trusted the keeper
behind them. Soon, Edin and Mohamed were
banging in the goals at one end, and Alisson was
stopping them at the other.

Against Astra Giurgiu, he dived bravely at
the striker's feet to block the first shot, and then
scrambled back up to make a second and then a
third block.

'Thanks mate, you really saved us there!' Juan
called out.

Having topped their group, Roma were through to the second round – the Round of 32 – and Alisson continued to show off his safe hands against Spanish club Villarreal. Mario Gaspar's flick header was flying into the bottom corner, but he reacted quickly to push the ball around the post.

'What a save!' Federico shouted above the roar of the Roma fans.

At the final whistle, Alisson had a clean sheet, Edin had a hat-trick, and Roma were through to the Europa League Last 16. Happy days!

Was Spalletti watching? Sadly, Alisson's cup performances didn't seem to make any difference. In Serie A, Wojciech was still Roma's Number 1.

'Will I always be the back-up?' Alisson wondered miserably. He thought about going to speak to Spalletti, but in the end he kept quiet. For now, he had to stay positive and patient, just like he had during his early days at Internacional. He had plenty more football to look forward to, starting with a Coppa Italia semi-final against Roma's local rivals, Lazio.

For Alisson, it was his first taste of the famous Rome Derby. Wow, what an atmosphere! As the teams walked out onto the pitch at the Stadio Olimpico, the Lazio fans waved their massive, light blue flags and chanted as loudly as they could. Alisson had never seen such passion, not even in the Brazilian national team.

'Time for me to shine,' he thought to himself, clapping his gloves together.

It turned out to be a busy night for Alisson.

He leapt to the left to tip Sergej Milinković-Savić's header wide. *SAVED!*

He threw himself to the right to stop Ciro Immobile's powerful strike. *SAVED!*

But just when Alisson was feeling unbeatable, Lazio attacked again and took the lead. This time, there was nothing he could do to stop Milinković-Savić from scoring. *1–0!*

'Nooooo!' Alisson groaned, looking down at his boots in disappointment.

And late in the second half, Lazio scored again. Keita Baldé raced down the right wing and crossed to Immobile, who slid the ball under a desperately diving Alisson. *2–0!*

'Game over,' he thought to himself glumly as he lay there in the back of his own net.

Roma were out of the Coppa Italia. Soon, they were out of the Europa League too; away at Lyon, Alisson didn't stand a chance against the French attackers, who were in lethal form.

'How am I supposed to stop that?' he asked himself as Alexandre Lacazette's shot rocketed into the top corner. *4–2!*

And with that, Alisson's first season at Roma was over. Fifteen games, nineteen goals conceded, four clean sheets, zero trophies and zero Serie A appearances. It hadn't been a brilliant success, but there was plenty for him to learn from his experiences. Now, Alisson needed to push on and become Roma's proper Number 1. There was no time to waste.

'The next World Cup is only a year away,' he reminded his family during the summer break. 'If I want to be Brazil's Number 1, I have to be playing every week. Otherwise, I'll need to leave!'

But as with his rapid rise with the national team, Alisson's situation changed very quickly at Roma. First, Spalletti left the club and Eusebio Di Francesco took over. Alisson got on well with his new manager, who liked his confident, sweeper-keeper style.

Then, Wojciech left too, to join their Italian rivals Juventus.

'No problem,' Di Francesco told his players ahead of the new Serie A season. 'Alisson was going to be my first-choice anyway!'

Suddenly, Alisson really was Roma's Number 1, and he even had the shirt to prove it.

CHAPTER 17

SERIE A'S STAR
KEEPER

In August 2017, a year after arriving at Roma, Alisson was all set to make his Serie A debut. An away trip to Atalanta was a tricky way to start, but with Number 1 on his back, he was raring to go. When the teams walked out onto the pitch, he was proud to be second in line behind Daniele Di Rossi, the captain.

'Let's win this!' Alisson cried, clapping and cheering as he took up his position in the penalty area.

Right, how could he help to make that happen? Alisson kept moving and talking and calling for the ball. The Roma players knew that they could pass it back to him whenever they needed.

'You're our fifth defender,' Juan liked to say. 'Our sweeper keeper!'

For the first thirty minutes, Alisson got involved in the game, but he didn't have too much goalkeeping to do. That all changed, however, when Aleksandar Kolarov gave Roma the lead with a clever free kick that went under the wall. *1–0!*

'Right, focus!' Alisson called out to his teammates. Things were about to get busy at the back.

Together, the Roma defence dealt with every danger. Juan blocked Andrea Petagna's strike, Aleksandar headed away a teasing cross, and Kostas closed down Papu Gómez before he had time to shoot.

'Great work, guys!' Alisson encouraged their efforts.

And if Atalanta did get through the Roma defence, Alisson was always there to save the day. He was growing more confident – and more commanding. He was so calm that he made everyone around him feel calm too. His teammates trusted his safe hands to handle anything, and so did Di Francesco, his manager.

At the final whistle, Alisson punched the air and

ran over to give Juan a big hug. A win and a clean sheet – what a start to the new Serie A season! And the clean sheets kept on coming.

Roma 3 Verona 0,

Benevento 0 Roma 4,

AC Milan 0 Roma 2,

Torino 0 Roma 1,

Roma 1 Crotone 0,

Roma 1 Bologna 0...

That was seven clean sheets in only their first eleven games! So Alisson and his defence were on fire going into their biggest game of the season so far: Lazio. It was time to get revenge in the Rome Derby.

With their fans cheering them on, Roma put on their best performance yet. Right from the kick-off, they fought for the ball and then pushed forward on the attack. Eventually, Diego Perotti scored a penalty and then Radja Nainggolan made it 2–0.

'Get in!' Was Alisson about to collect another clean sheet? He had barely made a save all game. But no, Lazio won a penalty and Immobile stepped up and scored. *2–1!*

117

'Argghh!' Alisson screamed up at the sky in frustration. He had dived the right way, but the ball had flown straight past him. So why hadn't he saved it? The shot had simply been too fast and forceful.

After a brief burst of anger, Alisson focused his mind on the match again. At least Roma were still winning – they just had to hold and keep working hard…

'Yessssss!' he bellowed as the final whistle blew at last.

The Roma players raced around the pitch, celebrating their well-deserved derby victory. Revenge was sweet, and suddenly, anything seemed possible, even winning the Serie A title. Roma had finished second the previous season, but weren't they now an even better team?

'Hey, if we keep winning, who knows what could happen?' Alisson told Federico with a shrug of his shoulders and a big smile on his face.

Sadly, Roma couldn't keep winning, but they did keep collecting clean sheets. It was becoming a normal thing now for Alisson and Co. They had the best defensive record in the league, even better than Wojciech's Juventus. So, could they secure a top-four finish?

Alisson was focused on achieving that aim. He would fight until the end, making save after save.

Away at Inter Milan, he played his greatest game of the season so far. After making a double save to deny Ivan Perišić, he spotted Stephan El Shaarawy making a run down the right wing. He was a long way away, but Alisson's accuracy was amazing.

PING! The pass landed just over the Inter defender's head and right into Stephan's path. *1–0!*

In his penalty area, Alisson threw his arms up triumphantly. He was very proud of his first Roma assist.

Right, that was his attacking work over – time to defend. Suddenly, though, the Roma backline found themselves under real pressure.

Mauro Icardi raced onto Milan Skriniar's through-ball… but out rushed Alisson to get there first.

Perišić's cross took a wicked deflection off Alessandro Florenzi's boot and was dipping towards the top corner... but up stretched Alisson to tip the ball away.

Antonio Candreva fired a fizzing shot through the crowded penalty area... but down dived Alisson to catch it safely in his gloves.

How had Inter still not scored an equaliser? Because Roma's great goalkeeper was unbeatable – that was why!

When the ball fell to Icardi at the back post, it looked like he would surely make it 1–1. He swivelled and shot... but at the last second, Alisson's right arm flew out to flick it onto the post.

No way! How had he done that? Was he human, or some kind of footballing wizard? It was an unbelievable save, his best of the season.

But despite Alisson's incredible keeping, Inter did score, and equalise, in the end. As he watched the ball finally fly past him, it felt like a kick to the stomach. Ouch! What a cruel blow after all that wonderful work. He was furious with his defenders. They had been so close to yet another crucial clean sheet!

Oh well, there would be other clean sheets to be celebrated in big games later that season:

Roma 3 Torino 0,

Lazio 0 Roma 0,

Roma 0 Juventus 0

That last difficult draw against Juventus was enough to earn Roma a third-place finish and a Champions League spot. Hurray!

But it was just another game for Alisson, in that he made saving the day look so simple. He hardly ever made mistakes these days, but especially not against his old rival. It was his seventeenth clean sheet of the season, whereas Wojciech at Juventus only had nine.

Yes, the Italian league had a new star keeper now, and although Roma didn't win a trophy that season, Alisson did – Serie A Goalkeeper of the Year.

CHAPTER 18

LIGHTING UP THE CHAMPIONS LEAGUE

Alisson wasn't just starring in Serie A during 2017–18, though. No, he was also lighting up the Champions League with his spectacular saves. He was winning his battles against the best attackers in the game.

In the group stage, Alisson kept out Antoine Griezmann's Atlético Madrid *and* Eden Hazard's Chelsea to help Roma finish top of the table. At home at the Stadio Olimpico, he was like a magical shot-stopping machine.

'How on earth did we not score?' their opponents were left wondering.

In the Last 16, Alisson saved the day again against

Shakhtar Donetsk. Roma lost the away leg 2–1, but it would have been much worse if it hadn't been for their great goalkeeper...

Alisson flew through the air like Superman to stop Taison's strike from going into the top corner. *SAVED!*

He threw up his strong right arm to block a certain goal for Marlos. *SAVED!*

In the final seconds, Shakhtar's striker Facundo Ferreyra found himself unmarked in the six-yard box, with what looked like an empty goal to aim at. What a chance to make it 3–1! But Roma's great goalkeeper wasn't giving up. As Ferreyra took the shot, Alisson scrambled across his goal and stretched out a desperate glove. Amazingly, he got his fingertips on the ball and flicked it off Bruno's boot, and over the crossbar. *SAVED!*

'Yes, we did it!' Alisson celebrated with his teammate. Together, they had somehow stopped Shakhtar from scoring a third.

That turned out to be a massive moment because Roma could only win the home leg 1–0. But thanks

to Alisson and Bruno, that was enough to take them
through on away goals.

'Quarter-finals, here we come!' the two Brazilians
cheered, arm in arm.

Alisson didn't want their exciting European
adventure to end, but things were about to get
a lot tougher. Roma's next opponents were
Barcelona. That meant Andrés Iniesta, Luis Suárez
and, of course, Lionel Messi, the best player on
the planet.

Some of the defenders were worried, but
Alisson stayed as calm and confident as ever. He was
ready for his ultimate challenge. Roberto Negrisolo,
his old coach at Roma, had recently called him
'The Messi of Goalkeepers'. It was time to see if
that was true.

'Come on, we can win this!' Alisson cheered.

On the away leg at the Nou Camp, he managed
to keep out Messi, but sadly not his Barcelona
teammates. Or his own teammates, in fact.

Daniele scored an unlucky own goal. *1–0!*

Then Kostas scored one too. *2–0!*

Alisson saved from Suárez, but Gerard Piqué tapped in the rebound. *3–0!*

Edin Džeko found the net eventually. *4–1!*

Game over? No, Roma's great goalkeeper wasn't giving up. There was still the home leg to come and they had an important away goal. Not only that, but back home at the Stadio Olimpico, they were unbeatable.

'We've won three out of our four games there, and we haven't let in a single goal!' Alisson reminded his Roma teammates.

It was going to take something very special to beat a team like Barcelona, but they had to keep believing. If Alisson could keep another clean sheet, then their attackers just needed to score three. It had to be the perfect performance, and it was.

In the sixth minute, Edin muscled his way through to get the first. *4–2!*

Suddenly, the Roma fans started to believe as much as their players did. Alisson had never heard so much noise in the Stadio Olimpico.

Early in the second-half, Daniele scored a penalty. *4–3!*

One more goal – that's all they needed now. Alisson didn't have much to do in defence, but he never stopped urging his teammates on.

'Keep going!'

'There's still time!'

With ten minutes to go, Cengiz Ünder curled a corner into the box and there was Kostas with a glancing header. *4–4!*

Suddenly, Alisson wasn't so calm anymore. He raced over to join the big team hug on the touchline. What a night it was turning out to be!

'Now we need to concentrate!' he called out once he was back in his box. Roma had ten tense minutes of defending to do.

Kostas cleared a cross from Ousmane Dembélé, and then another from Messi,

Federico blocked a shot from Suárez,

Alisson snatched the ball before Messi could shoot, and then raced out to tackle Piqué.

At last, it was all over. Roma had done it – they

had beaten Barcelona. They were through to the
Champions League semi-finals!

'What a win!' Alisson roared as Alessandro jumped
into his arms.

That night, Roma's heroes hardly slept. The
celebrations went on and on, in the stadium and
all across the city. Alisson felt so proud to be a part
of such a famous victory. With the adrenaline still
running through his body, he sat at home in the early
hours of the morning and watched the whole game
again on TV.

'Okay, it really did happen,' Alisson said to himself
with a smile. 'I'm glad it wasn't a dream!'

Once the Roma players had calmed down after
all that excitement, they focused on their next
opponents – Liverpool. Jürgen Klopp, Liverpool's
manager, was building a brilliant team. They now
had Virgil van Dijk leading from the back and
Alisson's old Roma teammate, Mohamed Salah,
starring in attack alongside Sadio Mané and Roberto
Firmino. They were quickly becoming one of the
most dangerous strike forces in the world.

But Alisson was ready and waiting. He didn't want his exciting European adventure to end at the semi-final stage either.

'We're so close to the final,' he reminded Kostas before kick-off at Anfield. The atmosphere was already amazing, like a big, bubbling pot of noise.

Roma started well, but they had to be careful about the quick counter-attack. Mohamed had always been fast and skilful, and now that he was at Liverpool, he was more lethal than ever. With his first shot, he tried to curl the ball into the far corner, but Alisson pushed it away to safety.

'Don't let Mo shoot with his left foot!' he screamed at his defenders.

But it was no use; Mohamed was unstoppable. Even a great goalkeeper like Alisson couldn't save his second shot that flew straight into the top corner. *1–0!*

Mohamed made it 2–0 just before half-time with a cheeky chip over Alisson. How humiliating! And Mohamed kept going, setting up goals for Mané and Firmino. *4–0!*

'You've got to get tighter to him! Why are you giving him so much space?' Alisson yelled at his defenders, waving his arms in frustration. For once, he was losing his battle against the best attackers in the game.

Game over? No, late on at Anfield, Roma managed to pull two goals back to make it 5–2. They couldn't pull off another incredible comeback at home at the Stadio Olimpico, could they?

Not quite, but they got very close. With ten minutes to go, they were 3–2 up on the night, and only 7–5 down on aggregate. And then in the very last seconds, Radja scored a penalty to make it 7–6.

'Come on, ref – please don't blow the whistle yet!' Alisson muttered under his breath. They only needed one more goal now – one more goal.

But sadly, Roma had run out of time. Their amazing European adventure was over. There would be no Champions League final for them.

'Hey, heads up,' Alisson told his disappointed teammates as he walked around the pitch, 'we did everything we could.'

Roma's great goalkeeper had certainly given it everything. And with every perfect performance, his reputation had grown and grown. Real Madrid wanted to sign a new keeper that summer, and Alisson was now top of their list, alongside Thibaut Courtois. And even if they went for Courtois instead, that would mean that Chelsea then needed a new Number 1. Plus, Liverpool were interested in signing him, too.

Alisson was going to have a difficult decision to make during the summer, but before that, there was a big trip to Russia. He had a World Cup to try and win, with Brazil.

CHAPTER 19

WORLD CUP 2018

Alisson had kept his place as Brazil's Number 1, just like he had promised himself. Even when things hadn't been going well at club level for Roma, he had continued to save the day for his country.

Early in the World Cup qualifier against their big rivals Argentina, Alisson made a save to keep out Lucas Biglia's long-range strike. With a leap and a stretch, he got a strong left glove on the ball and tipped it behind for a corner.

'What a stop, big man!' Marquinhos cried out, giving his heroic keeper a high-five.

After that scary moment, Brazil's forwards burst

into life, and Alisson's old Under-17 teammates took over.

Philippe cut in off the wing and hit a wonderstrike. *1–0!*

Neymar Jr broke through and slid a shot into the bottom corner. *2–0!*

Wow, Brazil were looking brilliant under their new coach, Tite – solid at the back and exciting in attack. They finished ten points clear at the top of the South American qualification table. Now, they just had to keep their fine form going at the 2018 World Cup.

For Alisson, it helped that he now had a serious rival for Brazil's Number 1 shirt. Ederson was playing excellently in the Premier League for Manchester City, and many fans thought that he deserved to start for Brazil instead.

'We'll see about that!' Alisson thought, upping his game.

Competing with Ederson felt like his brotherly battles with Muriel all over again. But it spurred him on and kept him motivated during the biggest year of his career. To play at the World Cup had always been Alisson's dream, ever since watching the 1998 tournament as a young boy with his family. Twenty years later, that dream was about to become a reality.

Alisson couldn't wait. After his amazing season at Roma, he was feeling confident. Brazil were one of the favourites to win the World Cup in 2018, along with Spain, Germany and France. Back home, the Brazilians were expecting huge things from their team. But as long as they stuck together and made the most of their talent, there was no reason why they couldn't lift the trophy again.

Once in Russia, Brazil started well in their first Group E game against Switzerland. In the twentieth minute, Philippe scored another screamer, and the *Seleção* were up and running. They seemed to be in total control of the game, but they couldn't find that second goal to secure the victory.

Still, with Alisson in goal, what could go wrong? Well, even the greatest goalkeepers can't do everything on their own. They have to trust their teammates to do their jobs.

As the corner came in, there were five defenders in Brazil's six-yard box and only one Swiss striker. But somehow, Steven Zuber still had a free header. *1–1!*

'Why weren't you watching him?' Alisson asked as the ball landed in the back of his net. One chance, one goal – that's what happened if they switched off, even for a second.

Casemiro and Miranda just looked at each other, and then down at the ground. There was nothing they could say.

Although there were still forty minutes left, Brazil failed to find a winning goal. The players were disappointed with the draw, but they only had themselves to blame. They would just have to do a lot better in their next two matches.

Fortunately, there would be no more mistakes for Brazil in Group E. Alisson didn't have to make a single save in the 2–0 win over Costa Rica, and he only had to make one save in their victory over Serbia. Two wins, two clean sheets – Brazil were back on track, and just in time for the knockout stage.

In the Round of 16, Alisson was a bit busier

when Brazil faced Mexico, whose attack had speed, skill and Javier Hernández to finish things off. But Brazil's Number 1 calmly dealt with every danger. He punched away crosses and tipped shots over the bar. Alisson wasn't taking any chances, not at a World Cup, not with his whole country counting on him. At the other end, Neymar Jr and Roberto Firmino scored the goals to send them through. Another win, another clean sheet – yes, everything was going according to plan for Brazil.

Next up, however, was Belgium. They had quality players all over the pitch, and especially in attack. Eden Hazard, Kevin De Bruyne, Romelu Lukaku – Alisson had watched enough Champions League football to know how dangerous those three could be.

'Keep your focus until the final whistle!' he warned his defenders.

But it just wasn't Brazil's day, or their World Cup. First, Thiago Silva's touch bounced off the Belgium post, and then five minutes later, Fernandinho flicked the ball into his own net. It flew past Alisson before he could really react. As he sat back up, he looked around at his teammates, totally speechless. What had just happened? And how?

Oh dear, that goal gave Belgium an extra boost. Lukaku picked up the ball deep in his own half and dribbled straight through the Brazil midfield. Eventually, he passed to De Bruyne, who fired a shot into the bottom corner. Again, Alisson had no chance of stopping it. *2–0!*

Uh oh, would Brazil be heading home at the quarter-final stage? What a disaster! To make matters worse for Alisson, it was happening against Courtois, the other keeper that Real Madrid were interested in signing. And the big Belgian was having an unbelievable game, making magical saves to stop Philippe and Neymar Jr. Suddenly, Alisson didn't look like the world's best keeper anymore.

Renato Augusto was at least able to make amends for Brazil with a goal, but with only fifteen minutes to go, and Belgium still in the lead, time was running out for Brazil…

'Up you go!' Tite called to Alisson when they won a late corner.

'Okay, boss!'

This was it – his big moment. Could Alisson save the day by scoring and become a national hero? No, because Neymar Jr took it before he had even arrived! That seemed to sum up Alisson's whole, frustrating tournament. Brazil were going home, but he just had to hope that there would be better World Cups to come.

CHAPTER 20

LEAVING FOR LIVERPOOL

With his World Cup sadly over, Alisson started thinking about his future at Roma. Did he want to stay for one more season to see if they could finally win a trophy together? Or was it best to move on like Mohamed?

That summer, Mohamed had messaged Alisson, urging his old teammate to join him at Liverpool. The Reds had a solid defence, a strong midfield, and a star strike force. All they needed now was a great goalkeeper.

'You're the missing piece!' Mohamed tried to persuade him.

After losing in the Champions League Final,

Liverpool had stepped up their search for a new Number 1. With the pressure on, Loris Karius had made two massive mistakes to hand the trophy to Real Madrid. It was so disappointing after all their hard work, but Klopp didn't panic. He carried on patiently building the best possible team, player by player. Mané, Wijnaldum, Salah, Robertson Van Dijk...

Who would be next? What he wanted was a calm keeper, with a safe pair of hands and skilful feet, who didn't make many mistakes...

'Mo's right – that's me!' Alisson thought to himself.

And Liverpool agreed. They had been keeping a close eye on him for years, ever since his early days at Internacional. Back then, there had been another Brazilian goalkeeper at Anfield, called Doni, who had recommended a promising young keeper who was about to break into the national team.

'Trust me, this guy's going to be great!' he had said.

When the Liverpool goalkeeping coach, John Achterberg, went to watch Alisson play, he was really impressed. 'He's perfect for the Premier League,' he thought straight away.

But at that time, the club had just signed Simon Mignolet from Sunderland for £9 million. There wasn't enough space for two top keepers. And so Alisson went to Roma instead, where he became a European star, keeping a whopping twenty-two clean sheets during the 2017–18 season. But now, after years of scouting, Liverpool were ready to make their move.

'He's the one I want!' Klopp told the club's owners.

At first, however, Roma stood firm. With Real Madrid and Chelsea also chasing after Alisson, they knew that they could charge a very high fee. Their starting price was... £90 million!

Alisson couldn't believe it, and neither could Liverpool. Wow – that was a lot of money to spend on one player, and especially a goalkeeper. In fact, it would be a new world record! So Liverpool had to say no.

'Okay, how about £75 million?' Roma suggested

instead, but that was still way too much for Liverpool to spend.

'No, let's look at other, cheaper options,' Klopp told his scouts. Really, there was only one great goalkeeper that he wanted, but maybe if they stopped showing interest in Alisson, Roma might lower their price...

That clever plan worked! Real Madrid chose Courtois, and Chelsea couldn't buy a new keeper until that deal was done. Suddenly, there weren't lots of teams competing to sign Alisson anymore. There was only one.

'Please talk to Liverpool again,' Alisson asked the Roma chairman. 'That's where I really want to go!'

Alisson had tried his best to forget that awful Champions League night at Anfield, when he had let in five goals, but he couldn't. He still remembered it all – the cheers from the Kop End, the electric atmosphere, and of course, the fast, attacking football. Under Klopp, Liverpool played the game in such an exciting way and this was Alisson's chance to be a part of it. The club already had an amazing history, but together, they could make even more! He was already thinking about all the trophies they would win…

At last, the two clubs agreed on a fee – £66.8 million. It was a lot cheaper than £90 million, but it still made him the most expensive goalkeeper ever.

'My bro, the record breaker!' teased Muriel, who was now playing in Europe too, for Belenenses in Portugal.

Alisson didn't care about a price-tag, though; the main thing was that he was on his way to Anfield! But first, he needed to say an emotional goodbye to everyone at Roma. The fans, the coaches, the players – he would miss them all so much. He would be forever grateful for their love and support.

Alisson arrived in England with great expectations on his shoulders. Was he really worth all that money? How much of a difference could one keeper make? Was he really going to help Liverpool lift the Champions League trophy and the Premier League title?

Some people had their doubts, but at Anfield, everyone was sure that they had signed a world-class keeper.

'He's a very calm person and a wonderful player,' Klopp told the media. 'Now we have everything we need for the season.'

As Alisson stood in front of the famous club badge, wearing the bright green goalie kit, he smiled and gave two thumbs up to the camera.

'I'm really happy, this is a dream come true!'

For now, Loris still had the Number 1 shirt, so Alisson would wear Number 13 instead. But it didn't really matter what it said on the back of his shirt. Everyone knew that he wasn't there to be the back-up; he was Liverpool's first-choice keeper now. He couldn't wait to start saving the day for his new club.

CHAPTER 21

ALMOST UNBEATABLE

Alisson's Premier League adventure began at Anfield in August 2018 – with a clean sheet! As hard as they tried, West Ham couldn't find a way past Liverpool's deadly defence, or their great new goalkeeper.

Alisson didn't have much saving to do, but he was always there if his teammates needed him. They trusted him with the ball already, even when there were strikers closing him down.

'Yes Virg, play it back!'

'I've got that, Joe!'

Every pass was played calmly and accurately, whether it was a gentle tap to one of his centre-backs or a long kick to the strikers. Liverpool's attacks started at the back with Alisson, and ended with goals for Mohamed, Sadio and Daniel Sturridge. 4–0 – job done!

And the wins and clean sheets kept coming:

Crystal Palace 0 Liverpool 2,

Liverpool 1 Brighton 0...

Away at Leicester, they were 2–0 up and cruising towards another comfortable victory. After making a couple of important stops, Alisson was feeling confident. Too confident, perhaps.

It all started with a poor back pass from Virgil, which put his keeper under real pressure. As Kelechi Iheanacho chased after him, Alisson thought about booting the ball far up the field and away from danger. But at the last second, he changed his mind.

Surely, he could do better than that. There had to be a pass that he could play, instead of just hoofing it away... But as he looked around for a teammate, the ball got stuck under his feet. He tried a Cruyff Turn, but Iheanacho tackled him. Oh no, Alisson had lost it and he was a long way from his goal.

As he raced back into position, Iheanacho crossed to Rachid Ghezzal, who fired the ball past his diving body. *2–1!*

'Noooo!' Alisson groaned, looking skywards, down on his knees. He had really let Liverpool down. It was a bad mistake and he only had himself to blame. Why hadn't he just cleared it straight away? It turned out that he was beatable, after all.

'Sorry guys,' Alisson apologised in the dressing room afterwards. He really hated making mistakes. 'I won't do that again. Ever!'

He was expecting Klopp to be angry with him, but he wasn't. 'Don't worry, these things happen sometimes when you play the way we play, attacking from the back. We still won the game, so there's no harm done. Besides, you're not the only one at fault for that goal. Your defenders didn't exactly make your life easy, did they? We can't expect you to be perfect every week!'

With his manager's support, Alisson went back to being almost unbeatable, just like Liverpool.

After seven games, The Reds were joint top of the Premier League table with Manchester City. It was time for the two teams to face each other at Anfield. It would also be a battle of the best Brazilian keepers: Alisson vs Ederson. Who would win?

The match was tight and tense, with few clear chances to score. But for the final fifteen minutes, Manchester City were on top, testing that deadly Liverpool defence.

Alisson dived down to stop Bernardo Silva's cross and then scrambled across his goal to save from Riyad Mahrez on the other side. As he got back up, Alisson could hear the fans chanting his name. It was nice to be busy for a change.

But just when the Liverpool fans had accepted a draw, Leroy Sané burst into the box and was fouled by Virgil. Penalty to Manchester City!

Now, Liverpool really needed their great new goalkeeper to save the day. Alisson had been a spot-kick king in the past back in Brazil; could he do it again at Anfield? He bounced from foot to foot, getting ready to leap at the last moment, just like he had practised with Daniel Pavan at Internacional.

Just as Mahrez struck the ball, Alisson made his move. He flew to his right, stretching his left arm high above his head, but the shot went sailing over the crossbar!

In a flash, the Liverpool captain Jordan Henderson was there hugging Alisson and calling him a hero.

'But I didn't save it,' he replied, 'Mahrez missed.'

Jordan just shrugged. 'You *made* him miss, mate!'

It was so far so good for Liverpool's season. Not only were they still in the Premier League title race; they were still in the Champions League too – and they really had Alisson to thank for that. With one game to go, Liverpool sat third in 'The Group of Death'. Neymar Jr's PSG were top of the table, but if The Reds could win at home against Napoli, they could still claim second place.

'Come on!' Jordan yelled as he led his team out onto the pitch.

With Anfield roaring them on, Liverpool took the lead in the first half, thanks to a goal from

Mohamed. Great, now they just had to hold on.
Alisson tightened his glove straps and got ready
for action.

'Focus!' he called out to his defenders.

The Napoli comeback took a long time to arrive,
but Alisson stayed alert until the very end, the
kind of concentration that made him such a great
goalkeeper. In injury time, José Callejón's cross
travelled all the way through to Arkadiusz Milik,
who was unmarked on the edge of the six-yard box.
Uh oh, Liverpool were in big, big trouble...

But at the last moment, Alisson rushed out
bravely, making his body as big as possible.
Although he stretched his arms out wide, he
actually stopped the shot with his legs. *SAVED!*

What an unbelievable block! Anfield roared again
– they had a new hero. That's why Liverpool had
paid so much money for him.

Once the ball had been cleared away, Alisson
allowed himself a quick celebration. A supersave
like that felt just as good as scoring a winning goal.

At last, the final whistle blew. Thanks to their

great goalkeeper, Liverpool were through to the Champions League Last 16.

'No-one can stop us now!' Alisson cheered, punching the air with passion. He was determined to end his first Liverpool season with at least one trophy.

CHAPTER 22

CHAMPIONS OF EUROPE

At the end of 2018, Liverpool were seven points clear at the top of the league. With their team looking so comfortable, the fans began to dream of a first-ever Premiership title. Was this going to be their season at last? They had been waiting so long – nearly twenty-seven years!

But bit by bit, Liverpool let that lead slip away. First, they lost to Manchester City and then they followed that up with a series of frustrating draws:

Liverpool 1 Leicester City 1,

West Ham 1 Liverpool 1,

Liverpool 0 Manchester United 0,

Everton 0 Liverpool 0

At the back, Alisson was doing everything he could to win, but the problem was at the other end of the pitch. Suddenly, Liverpool's attackers just weren't scoring enough goals.

'Hey, this isn't over yet,' Klopp told his disappointed team. 'Come on, City are only one point ahead of us, with nine games to go. We can still catch them!'

Liverpool soon got back to winning ways, but every time they picked up all three points, so did Manchester City.

'Not again!' Alisson moaned when Pep Guardiola's team squeezed past Leicester City, thanks to a thunderstrike from Vincent Kompany.

As both teams prepared for the final day of the season, there was still just that one point between them: 95 for Manchester City, 94 for Liverpool. After all their hard work, were they really going to lose the title like that? It seemed so unfair.

'First, we need to beat Wolves,' Klopp tried to focus his players before kick-off, 'and then we can worry about whether City beat Brighton, okay?'

Liverpool listened to their manager and won their match 2–0. Unfortunately for them, however, City won too. There was a strange atmosphere at Anfield as the players walked around the pitch after the final whistle. Because despite everything that the team had achieved together, they had missed out on the Premier League title by a single point.

Thankfully though, their season didn't end there. Virgil was named PFA Player of the Year and Alisson collected the Golden Glove Award for the most clean sheets: twenty-one. That was the highest number since 2005, and most importantly, one more than his Brazilian rival, Ederson.

Still, what Alisson wanted most was a team trophy, and Liverpool had one last chance to win one. For the second year in a row, they were through to the final of Europe's greatest club competition – the Champions League.

'Come on!'

Alisson and his teammates were so excited. It hadn't been an easy journey, and that made it all the more enjoyable. To reach the final, Liverpool had pulled off one of the most incredible comebacks in football history. For Alisson, it was the second time he had beaten Barcelona, but this one was even better than the win with Roma.

In the first leg at the Nou Camp, Liverpool lost 3–0, with Messi scoring two late goals. Some supporters feared that was game over, but not the players. They weren't giving up. Anything could happen back at Anfield.

'We can do this!' Sadio assured his teammates. Mohamed and Roberto were both out injured, but their fighting spirit was still there.

It would have to be a perfect Liverpool performance, however. In attack, they needed to score at least three goals, and at the back, they needed to keep another clean sheet.

'No problem,' Alisson said, staying as calm and confident as ever. With a great goalkeeper and such amazing defenders around him, they still had a chance.

Anfield was buzzing as the big game kicked off. What Liverpool needed was a strong start and an early goal...

In the sixth minute, Jordan burst into the Barcelona box. His shot was saved, but Divock Origi scored the rebound. *3–1!*

Game on! With his teammates pushing forward on the attack, Alisson had to be extra alert at the back.

He jumped up to tip a Messi strike over the bar,

He dived down to push away a shot from his Brazil teammate, Philippe,

And he rushed out to stop Jordi Alba from scoring.

'Nice one!' Jordan said, patting his brilliant keeper on the back.

At half-time, it was so far so good for Liverpool. They were 1–0 up and there was no need to panic yet. They still had forty-five minutes to score at least two more goals...

Early in the second half, Trent Alexander-Arnold crossed to super sub Gini Wijnaldum, who fired the ball in. *3–2!*

Then two minutes later, Gini scored again with a header. *3–3!*

'Yesssss!' Alisson cheered on the edge of his penalty area. Now, as Barcelona fought back, it was his time to shine, saving fierce shots from Suárez and then Messi.

'Great work!' Virgil cheered, giving his keeper a high-five.

The match was heading for extra-time, but what if Liverpool could score one more? With fifteen minutes to go, Trent caught Barcelona out with a quick corner-kick. He crossed it to Origi, who banged the ball into the top corner first time. *4–3!*

'YESSSSS!' Alisson was desperate to join in his team's joyful celebrations, but he decided to wait until after the final whistle. For now, he needed to stay focused on keeping that clean sheet.

It was a very tense last ten minutes at Anfield. Barcelona delivered lots of crosses into the Liverpool box, but out came Alisson to catch the ball and calm things down.

'Hurray!' the fans cheered. They were so pleased to have such a safe pair of hands in goal now.

At last, the final whistle blew. What a comeback! Alisson raced over to Virgil, who lifted him high into the air.

'We did it! We did it!' the Liverpool players cheered together. It was a night that none of them would ever forget.

But now, it was time for the biggest game of them all – the 2019 Champions League final. The Liverpool players were rested and ready; this time, they were going to win, not lose. It would be them, surely – not their opponents Tottenham – lifting the trophy at the end.

'Let's do this!' Alisson called out, clapping his gloves together.

They had beaten Tottenham twice in the Premier League that season, but he had conceded a goal in each game. Not this time, though. He was going to keep a clean sheet against Harry Kane and Co. He was sure of it.

Liverpool took the lead in only the second minute in Madrid, thanks to a penalty from Mohamed. What a start! But they didn't just sit back and defend after that. No, they kept playing the way they always played, attacking from the back.

Alisson got the ball and calmly passed it forward to

Joël Matip, who played it out to Robbo as he raced down the left wing. The Tottenham keeper Hugo Lloris could only tip his shot over the bar for a corner.

'That's it – keep going!' Alisson cheered from his goal.

It was only really in the last ten minutes that Alisson had to step up and save the day for Liverpool.

He got two strong hands on Son Heung-min's strike and pushed the ball away from the danger zone. *SAVED!*

He got down low to catch Lucas Moura's shot. *SAVED!*

He leapt to the left to keep out Christian Eriksen's curling free kick. *SAVED!*

'Come on, we're so close now!' Alisson yelled at his tired teammates.

At last, in the eighty-seventh minute, Origi scored a second goal for Liverpool. Game over!

Well, not quite over, at least not for Alisson. He still wanted that clean sheet, to go with his Champions League winner's medal. And after a few more saves, he had it.

'Yesssss!' Alisson screamed, raising both arms in the air.

What a feeling! Liverpool players were hugging each other all over the pitch, crying tears of pure joy. This was what they had been working so hard to win. Now, they had done it – they were the new Champions of Europe!

As Jordan lifted the trophy high into the sky, Alisson sat at the front of the stage, enjoying every magical moment.

CHAPTER 23

BRILLIANT FOR BRAZIL

The Premier League Golden Glove and now the
Champions League trophy – what a year 2019 was
turning out to be for Alisson! And even though the
club season was now over, he still had shots to save
for his country, and a cup to compete for.

The Copa América was about to start and this
time, Brazil were the hosts as well as the favourites.
That meant there was even more pressure on the
Seleção to perform well. After two embarrassing
World Cup exits and two dreadful Copa América
displays, it was about time that Brazil won a
tournament again.

'That's right!' their Number 1 agreed. The year

2019 had belonged to Alisson, and so it had to be Brazil's year too. Sadly, Neymar Jr was out injured, but all of their other attacking stars were available – Philippe, Willian, Gabriel Jesus, Richarlison, and of course, his Liverpool teammate, Roberto.

However, it was in defence that Brazil looked strongest. Dani Alves, Marquinhos, Thiago Silva, Filipe Luís, and behind them, Alisson. What a brilliant backline! It was going to take something very special to beat them.

Although Bolivia tried their best, Alisson was alert to any danger.

Brazil 3 Bolivia 0

Venezuela created a few more chances, but nothing that Alisson couldn't handle.

Brazil 0 Venezuela 0

After a strong start, Peru fell apart.

Brazil 5 Peru 0

Hurray! Brazil were through to the Copa América quarter-finals, and Alisson had kept three clean sheets already.

But scoring goals proved a big problem for

Brazil against Paraguay. Even though they were playing against ten men for the last thirty-five minutes, it was still 0–0, and so the match went to penalties.

Luckily, Brazil had a spot-kick king as their keeper. Alisson was feeling confident, especially after making some good saves in the game. This was his time to shine like his heroes Taffarel and Dida.

Gustavo Gómez went first for Paraguay, and Alisson guessed the right way. Diving low to his left, he pushed the ball powerfully away. *SAVED!*

As the home crowd went wild around him, Alisson calmly got back up to his feet and walked to the side. No big deal! Nine spot-kicks later, Brazil were on their way through to the semi-finals.

'Yes, you legend!' Gabriel cried out as he jumped into Alisson's arms.

He was happy to be his nation's hero, but he wasn't getting carried away just yet. 'We have to keep working,' Alisson told the media afterwards – because next up for Brazil were Messi and Agüero's

Argentina. It was the match that everyone had been waiting for – South America's top two teams going head to head. So, who would make it through to the Copa América Final?

Brazil, of course – it was Alisson's year! In their biggest game, they were back to their brilliant best. They battled hard for every ball, working together as a team. Their defence stood strong, and their attack scored goals again.

In the first half, Roberto set up Gabriel. *1–0!*

Then in the second, Gabriel set up Roberto. *2–0!*

'Well done, we did it!' Alisson celebrated at the final whistle, punching the air with both fists.

Brazil were through to the Copa América Final and Alisson still hadn't been beaten. Not once! In total, that was nine clean sheets in a row, for club and country. Could Alisson make it ten? He would give it his best shot.

Their opponents would be Peru, the team they had thrashed 5–0 in the group stage. So, were Brazil all set to become South American champions for a ninth time? No, finals were never that simple.

'Let's just play like we did against Argentina,' the players agreed, 'and we can think about lifting the trophy later!'

Gabriel crossed to Everton. *1–0!*

The Maracanã Stadium shook with the sound of 60,000 Brazilians celebrating. Their team were on the verge of another tournament victory. But just before half-time, Thiago Silva slipped and handballed it in the box. *Penalty to Peru!*

Oh well, if he wanted that tenth clean sheet, Alisson would just have to save it, like he had in the shoot-out against Paraguay. He dived down to his right, but Paolo Guerrero's shot rolled into the opposite corner. *1–1!*

'Nooooo!' After five-and-a-half games, Alisson had finally been beaten, but it didn't take Brazil long to bounce back. In the final minute of the first half, Arthur passed to Gabriel, who poked it past the keeper. *2–1!* It stayed that way until the ninetieth minute, when Richarlison scored to make it three.

164

Brazil were the new Copa América Champions! Their proud players danced around the pitch together in a big huddle. It had been a real team effort.

Campeones, Campeones, Olé! Olé! Olé!

As he kissed the trophy and lifted it high above his head, Alisson hoped that 2019 would never end. After all those years of dreaming and battling with his brother, he had finally reached football's highest level. He was Brazil's Number 1, and Liverpool's too, lifting the Copa América and the Champions League. Not only that, but he had also won:

the Premier League Golden Glove for being the best keeper in England,

the Champions League Goalkeeper of the Year award for being the best in Europe,

and now the Copa América Golden Glove for being the best in South America.

So, it was official – Alisson was now the greatest goalkeeper in the whole world! And at the age of twenty-six, he still had so many successful years ahead of him. There was so much more that he wanted to achieve, starting with the Premier League title with Liverpool, and ending, one day hopefully, with the World Cup for Brazil.

Internacional
🏆 Campeonato Gaúcho: 2013, 2014, 2015, 2016

Liverpool
🏆 UEFA Champions League: 2018–19
🏆 FIFA Club World Cup: 2019

Brazil U23s
🏆 Toulon Tournament: 2013

Brazil
🏆 Copa América: 2019

Individual

🏆 Serie A Goalkeeper of the Year: 2017–18

🏆 Serie A Team of the Year: 2017–18

🏆 Premier League Golden Glove: 2018–19

🏆 UEFA Champions League Goalkeeper of the

🏆 Season: 2018–19

🏆 Copa América Golden Glove: 2019

🏆 UEFA Team of the Year: 2019

🏆 The Best FIFA Goalkeeper: 2019

🏆 Yashin Trophy: 2019

ALISSON

① THE FACTS

NAME: Alisson Ramses Becker

DATE OF BIRTH: 02 October 1992

AGE: 27

PLACE OF BIRTH: Novo Hamburgo

NATIONALITY: Brazil

BEST FRIEND: His brother Muriel

CURRENT CLUB: Liverpool

POSITION: GK

THE STATS

Height (cm):	191
Club appearances:	258
Club goals:	0
Club trophies:	6
International appearances:	44
International goals:	0
International trophies:	1
Ballon d'Ors:	0

★ ★ ★ HERO RATING: 89 ★ ★ ★

GREATEST MOMENTS

8 JUNE 2013,
BRAZIL 1–0 COLOMBIA

Alisson bounced back from failure at the 2009
Under-17 World Cup to win the 2013 Toulon
Tournament with Brazil. Except for one early mistake
against Belgium, Alisson was unbeatable, keeping
three classy clean sheets on the way to lifting his first
international trophy.

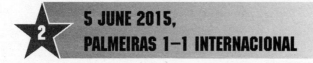

5 JUNE 2015, PALMEIRAS 1–1 INTERNACIONAL

During Alisson's breakthrough season at Internacional, his team reached the Brazilian Cup quarter-finals. Not only did his saves keep them in this game, but Alisson also saved a penalty from Palmeiras striker Lucas Barrios. With the national team coach watching, it wasn't long before he became Brazil's Number 1.

10 APRIL 2018, ROMA 3–0 BARCELONA

After losing the first leg 4–1, Roma looked like they were crashing out of the Champions League in the quarter-finals. But no, back home at the Stadio Olimpico, they pulled off an incredible comeback. Edin Džeko, Daniele De Rossi and Kostas Manolas got the goals in attack, while Alisson kept out Messi and Suárez at the back.

1 JUNE 2019, LIVERPOOL 2–0 TOTTENHAM

This wasn't the greatest Champions League Final ever, but the result was all that mattered. After losing the previous year against Real Madrid, Liverpool were the new Champions of Europe! This time, Alisson was their safe hands at the back, keeping another clean sheet to go with his winner's medal.

27 JUNE 2019, BRAZIL 0–0 PARAGUAY (WON 4–3 ON PENALTIES)

Alisson only conceded one goal all tournament as Brazil won the 2019 Copa América, and that was a penalty against Peru in the final. But he played his best game in the quarter-final against Paraguay. After making some super stops during the match, Alisson then saved a penalty during the shoot-out to become his country's hero.

PLAY LIKE YOUR HEROES

SAVE THE DAY LIKE ALISSON

STEP 1: Don't switch off, not even for a second.

STEP 2: Watch the action calmly and carefully, alert to any signs of a counter attack… Right, ready to save the day?

STEP 3: If your opponents try a throughball, rush out to deal with the danger. Just make sure that you get there first, though!

STEP 4: If your opponents cross the ball into the box, jump up bravely to catch it if you can. If not, punch it powerfully up the pitch.

STEP 5: And if your opponents go for goal, this is your time to really shine. Use your agility to fly through the air and stop the shot. Then use your arm strength to push the ball away, as far and as wide as possible.

STEP 6: Hopefully, you've cleared the danger, but be ready to spring back up, just in case. You might need to save the day for a second time.

TEST YOUR KNOWLEDGE

QUESTIONS

1. How did Alisson's dad celebrate Brazil reaching the 1998 World Cup Final?

2. Who was Brazil's Number 1 at the 2002 World Cup?

3. Where did Alisson and Muriel's 1 vs 1 brotherly battles take place?

4. Which two Brazilian superstars did Alisson first play with at the 2009 Under-17 World Cup?

5. When Alisson made his debuts for both Internacional and Brazil, who was the manager on both occasions?

6. Which two legendary Brazilian goalkeepers helped Alisson during his early career?

7. How many Italian league matches did Alisson play during his first season at Roma?

8. How many goals did Alisson let in when Roma played Liverpool at Anfield in 2018?

9. Which ex-Roma teammate urged Alisson to join Liverpool?

10. Alisson kept twenty-one Premier League clean sheets during the 2018–19 season, beating which other Brazilian keeper by one?

11. How many goals did Alisson let in for Brazil at the 2019 Copa América?

Answers below. . . No cheating!

1. By dunking his face in a cake! 2. Marcos 3. All in their living room at home 4. Philippe Coutinho and Neymar Jr 5. Dunga 6. Taffarel and Dida 7. Zero! 8. Five 9. Mohamed Salah 10. Ederson 11. One – and it was a penalty in the final!